The Love that Will Not Let You Go

The Love that Will Not Let You Go

Being Christian is Not What You Think

Douglas Heidt

WIPF & STOCK · Eugene, Oregon

THE LOVE THAT WILL NOT LET YOU GO
Being Christian is Not What You Think

Wipf & Stock
An Imprint of Wipf and Stock Publishers
199 W. 8th Ave., Suite 3
Eugene, OR 97401

www.wipfandstock.com

ISBN 13: 978-1-4982-0351-7

Manufactured in the U.S.A.   05/04/2015

To Mary V.

With gratitude for a foundation well laid

Blest be the Tie

O Love that wilt not let me go,
I rest my weary soul in Thee;
I give Thee back the life I owe,
That in Thine ocean depths its flow
May richer, fuller be.

—George Matheson, 1882

Contents

Acknowledgments

THE PEOPLE AND EXPERIENCES that have helped formulate these ideas are legion. I take ownership for the conclusions herein, but I am grateful for searchers who have gone before, whose dedication and careful study have fed me in bringing these concepts into focus.

I appreciate all the pastors, educators, church people, and others who opened my eyes and heart to a Loving God. I am grateful to my teachers at Davidson College and Union Presbyterian Seminary in Richmond, VA, who opened my mind to critical thinking and reinforced the joy of reading and learning. In particular, I thank my family: my wife Sharon, our daughter Kathryn and her husband Reuben, our son Daniel and his wife Diane, as well as my brothers, Alan and Sid, for their encouragement and support, and the contributions from their incisive minds. Many of the ideas and discoveries herein rose from their lives and experiences. I wish to thank my colleague and friend since seminary days, Dean Thompson, pastor and recently retired president of Louisville Presbyterian Seminary; Gay Mothershed, educator, executive, and former vice moderator of the Presbyterian General Assemby; Forrest Palmer, pastor, presbytery executive, and president of the Association of Presbyterian Church Educators; Don Campbell, pastor, teacher, retired executive in the Presbyterian Church Office of Professional Development; and seminary classmate Charlie Davidson, pastor, author, and psychotherapist. These are among scores of valued friends who have made inestimable contributions and encouragement to the development of these pages.

I am indebted to the congregations I have served, and especially to the First Presbyterian Church of Charleston, WV, with the remarkable and vast array of inquisitive minds, opinions, and points of view of members, attendees, classes, groups, and staff, that over the years join unbreakably together in living and exercising constantly the Love of Jesus Christ, in the church family and around the world. The Thursday morning Bible study group has been indispensable for me in discovering, sharpening, and correcting my thoughts, and a unique experience for personal support for all of us.

The work would never have been finished without the help of the people at Quinn Computer, the patient computer assistance of Nellie Howard, and the editorial and computer skills of Leslie Curtis, who spent hours with the manuscript, and whose cheerful assistance and guidance I greatly appreciate. And finally, thanks to my friend and fishing buddy Doug Propst, who, having read the manuscript reported, "I Love it! You're going straight to hell!"

I have thoroughly enjoyed nourishing these ideas to fruition, and look forward to how they continue to grow in the future.

Doug Heidt
Easter 2015

1

Who I Am

As I write this, I see out my back window that a green spring is beginning to appear in the winter of these West Virginia hills. A couple of deer make their way through the still mostly bare trees in the woods at the edge of the yard. Our dog is around the corner of the house. She knows they're there, and they know she knows. I think they've called an uneasy truce, for she couldn't catch them if she tried. But, her legs tremble in her sleep and she still dreams of the chase. And in the sheltering trees, always alert, watching, the deer will take no chances.

Along with life's breathtaking beauty and cherished moments of miraculous Love, the world is full of danger, fear, and enemies. Swords are sharpening in the Middle East, Americans by the thousands are arming themselves, nations still lift up swords against nations, and violence is everywhere. Across the globe the chasm between the haves and the have-nots swells, and greed is rampant. The words of candidates and election campaigns that seem endless are designed to evoke fear and hatred in the land, hoping they will turn into votes. In every land, children by the millions wander the streets lost, alone, afraid. I have lost some good friends to death over the winter. Bad things happen to good people, and good things happen to bad. People everywhere are hungry for food and clean water, honest work, security, and life. They yearn for happiness, justice, fair play, and peace. The winter has been cold and dreary. It had its own strange beauty, and the skiers loved it, but I'm glad it's done. Winter things happen in every season, but spring seems to me to have a healing beauty, and it is near. It's a reminder of all things coming.

Since the beginning, in all kinds of religious and philosophical systems, humankind has tried to make sense of life and its seasons, its darkness and light, peace and war, comfort and pain, success and failure, grief and joy, birth, life, death, good and evil, hate and Love. I have been a Presbyterian pastor for nearly half a century, and I have lived and walked with people through all these and more, and I can't help but feel their struggle and their joy. I am writing this because, after a lifetime of searching, this is what I have come to affirm is the truth about the struggles and celebrations of our life together, and the Love that is the substance of every truly joyful life. Year after year, I have read books and discussed ideas and asked questions and listened to sermons and lectures and studied journals and articles and listened in and out of churches. Now, as valuable and influential as all that has been, I am putting the books and papers down, and will try to articulate what in this world I conclude is holy and life-giving, and what truly makes sense.

After all these years, I am a Christian still, and I consider my conclusions to be Christian. For many, this will be pretty ordinary stuff, while for others some of it may be a departure, perhaps somewhat challenging, and outside the box. I believe what I have written is an accurate representation of Christian truth and the substance of the church's proclamation (or what I believe it should be). It seems important to me to write it as clearly and honestly as I can for my grandchildren, the rest of my family, all whom I know and Love, and those I Love but have yet to meet (including those who have left the church or the faith, or have never experienced either). This is for their comfort, their encouragement, and their joy. I want them to know that there are alternatives to much of what passes for Christianity on television, in movies, in videos, in political campaigns, and, I'm sorry to say, in many churches.

Whether you are an active Christian church member, or you are a seeker with real doubts and sometimes secret questions, or you simply consider yourself spiritual but not religious, or you just don't really care one way or another about all this religious stuff that doesn't seem to make much sense anyway, I invite you to come along for the ride. I invite you to consider what the Christian faith looks like from a slightly different, refocused angle. Read on, my friend, and discover that being Christian isn't what you think, it's what you do.

These thoughts came together and were written at a moment in time that has turned out to be an ongoing journey. I am constantly discovering new ways to express all these ideas, reforming and expanding them, and I expect that to continue. To that end, I seriously welcome your suggestions, questions, agreements, disagreements, and your critical thinking, in the true meaning of that concept.

I accept that you may or may not immediately affirm what I affirm here about the Christian faith. In fact, it has taken me a long time to get this far. But I give you these pages hoping that over time some interesting conversations and insights may result from them and a deeper truth emerge.

2

Where I'm Coming From

God is Love

*God is Love, and those who abide in Love abide
in God, and God abides in them.*[1]

God = Love

MIGHT AS WELL BEGIN at the beginning, on a sunny Sunday morning, when I was five or six years old. That was 1947, and everybody I knew went to church. I walked into my Sunday school classroom, not a care in the world, when a teacher (I remember her towering over me, stern and mountainous) grabbed my arm just above the elbow, pulled me up, got right in my face, and with a voice like the crack of doom, announced to me, "Now Listen!"

I did.

"We're not going to behave this morning like we did last week, are we?" she said.

I had no desire to argue the point, since I had no idea what we had done last week (I was certainly capable of having done *something*, and no doubt I did—probably arguing some theological

---

1. 1 John 4:16

4

point). In those days, at least where I lived, when an adult, especially at church, called you on your behavior, you got your act together, or your parents would find out about it, and that was never—I repeat, *never*—a desired consequence.

"No ma'am," I said, and hung my head in the best imitation of shame I could muster. For what, I never learned.

It is always possible that memories of such passing events (for I was capable of evoking multiple such corrective efforts) in my small child life might have nagged at me over time enough to turn me against church, Sunday school, religion, the whole story. That one harsh moment could have begun to teach me, as it has for many of us, that God is like a big, intimidating, angry Sunday school teacher—either an object of paralyzing dread, or simply not worth the trouble.

But, from my earliest memories, I was fortunate that in my church life beyond that morning, in my immediate and large extended family, friends, and other early experiences, Love and care had already filled my young life. It was already wrapped securely around me so that I was ready to hear what turned out to be the most significant theological manifesto I have ever known, and the key to this book. It was a song we sang almost every Sunday morning, year after year, until we could no longer consider ourselves "little children." If you did the Sunday school thing, you may have sung it too. In some places I think they still do. It's very simple. It went like this:

> Praise Him, praise Him, all you little children,
> God is Love, God is Love;
> Praise Him, praise Him, all you little children,
> God is Love, God is Love.[2]

I was given that song, and I have always remembered it and treasured it. God is Love! Before I knew what the word "insight" meant, I had one! The Love I already knew about was God. Before I knew about God, I knew Love. I have come to realize that the gift of Love, the capacity and the will to Love, the orientation of life

2. Forbes, ed., *Baptist Hymnal*, 31

around Love, and giving Love away are the most important things in all creation. I am convinced that the Spirit of God, truth breathing into me from beyond myself, was working in my experience, and made that Love real and visible.

Love is *right*; the most *right* thing there is in human life. I came to understand that God was not intimidating or angry after all; God is Love. The unnamed Love I already knew, and had known for a long time, was God.

Sounds like just pure sentimentality, doesn't it? Maybe even a little sappy. But stay with me on this. The song was right!

Love, indeed, won. It was not that I made a choice between the two— an angry God out to get me, or God as Love—and chose the latter (whoopee for me). Rather, through a growing awareness, reflecting on my life story and the stories of others, I have come to see that it is Love—Loving and being Loved, giving Love away— that is the most determinative element of all human experience.

You don't have to be a religious, churchgoing person (or even Christian) to know Love, and how it is the deepest and most profound element of human life. Churches have a particular language and stories and vocabulary to talk about Love, but it is not the only place where it exists. It is obvious that non-religious persons have Loved and do Love, and Love sacrificially. This Love in some or all its forms is the one experience that transcends and joins together every human life in every age and in every worldview.

Certainly not all persons have positive experiences of Love, and some have no experience of it at all. All of us have experienced the apparent absence of Love in our lives at one time or another. Countless people are tragically lacking in much Love at all, as their lives move slowly on, day by day, filled instead with sadness, hatred, frustration, depression, violence, and anger. Love is defined differently in different cultures. It is defined differently within cultures, as well. But among all of life's dynamics, Love, or the lack of it, or the yearning for it, is universally present. The tension between hatred and Love, between disinterest and Love, between ridicule and Love, between rejection and Love, between Love and the apparent absence of it, is the primary substance of life everywhere.

Love or the lack of it, or the distortion of it, or the celebration of it, constitutes the most basic component of human life. We all want it, we all are afraid of it, we all think we know how it should look in every human life everywhere, and we all revel in it when we are filled to overflowing with it. It is the deepest, brightest, most far-reaching, and most determinative experience that we—the whole human family—can know.

The experience of Love itself, in all its faces —healing, caring, supportive Love; Love that is persistent, sacrificial, forgiving, and universal —is what is required to deal with life's struggle against the forces that deny the experience of true joy. It is Loving-kind-ness —not right doctrine or belief, not self-esteem or success, not the right church or right kind of worship, not right politics or any one political system, not bank accounts or supreme power—but Love itself that yields a deeply joyful, authentic, completed life.

Now this next sentence would be a good one to highlight:

The Love you've just been reading about is, in reality, God.

It isn't that it's just *from* God, or *like* God, or a *reminder* of God. Love is in fact what God is.

This means that God is not out to get me, to crush me, to frighten, punish, or hurt me in some way if I don't behave or if I don't believe the right things or don't go to church enough.

God, as the song goes, is Love.

That's it. That's all. That's enough.

It's a good thing, too, because if my personal history follow-ing my encounter with the Sunday school sheriff that morning is any indication, my chances of screwing things up from time to time are still pretty good.

Love = God

Now this is important, so pay attention: I suggest that these two words, God and Love, in our religious language, are *interchangeable.*

Love, in fact, can be embraced as God's other name. No matter who you are or what your religion is, or even if you don't have one, this is worth remembering:

When you experience Love, you are experiencing God.

"God is Love," that is, "Love is God," is the core and essence of all we affirm as Christians, and is at the center of the Christian faith.

"But," you may say, "surely not *all* 'love' is God." And you would be right. There is a difference between Love and love. Sometimes it is not immediately discernible, and sometimes it takes a Loving fellowship with others to find that difference. There are times when what pretends to be Love is in fact manipulative, selfish, intentionally used to inflict pain, or designed to seize power or control. Then, of course, it is not Love. Love appears different in different cultures and settings, and it is not always immediately clear. But when you meet Love, when you sense God who is Love near you, when you feel the Spirit, the breath of God, breathing Love in you, that experience becomes your illumination and your awakening to a new life.

According to a 2008 Pew Research Center report, the fastest growing religious demographic group in the U.S. is made up of those who have rejected church ("organized" religion) and, for the most part, religion and religious practices in general. At last count, nearly 33 percent of Americans ages 18–25 are in this group, up from 25 percent in just five years.[3] Churches have tried to reach these people (and all people) with a "message." "But," we tell ourselves, "they just don't get it!" I believe they don't get it because we have been using our traditional language, while they speak a different language altogether. We have been speaking to them with religious/theological words, phrases, stories, and concepts that we have used for generations. They come naturally to us, such as, "You are saved by the blood of Jesus," "Jesus died for your sins," "Just believe," "Have faith," "Just talk to God about it," "Just Love Jesus and believe in him and obey the Ten Commandments, and you'll

---

3. Pew Forum, "'Nones' on the Rise"Executive Summary.

be fine," and "If you just have faith you'll get everything you ask for!" or "If you work hard enough and follow Jesus, heaven will be your big reward!" I get the feeling sometimes that we speak without listening to ourselves, and that when we do listen, *we are not sure we always fully understand what we ourselves are saying.* This is why it is so hard for churches, including many "evangelicals," to get their members to talk to other people about their faith.[4]

All this is a problem of language and translation. We are speaking a different language from those we are trying to reach. I once spent a few days with a family in Germany, and the beautiful four-year-old twin girls could only speak German. So they spoke to me in German very slowly, louder and louder. As when we meet someone who doesn't speak our language, the church tends to speak louder and slower in order to be understood. But turning up the volume of the message is not the problem. The problem is the language we use to speak the message. Regardless of whatever truth is in them, we are using too many words that people cannot comprehend or have already rejected and ignored. As membership in churches has declined steadily since the 1960s, science and technology have grown like wildfire, and to varying degrees they are the language of those who are unaffiliated with any religion. My conversations with people who have left the church or have never been a part of it tell me that it has gotten to the point that we are asking them to check their scientific understanding of the world at the church door, and use *our* language and concepts instead. They just can't do that.

Part of the solution begins with translation, finding a point of identifiable connection to bring the Christian faith into clear and simple focus, as when you put on glasses for the first time, and what you didn't even realize was blurry gives way to a world you never knew was so beautiful and clear. That clarity, that connection, is found when we use God's *other* name (as in, "God is Love").

When we say we want people to know God, we really mean we want people to know *Love*.

4. Pew Forum, "U.S. Religious Landscape Survey: Religious Beliefs and Practices," 51.

When we say God walked among us as Jesus, we actually mean *Love* itself walked among us.

When we say we want to follow God's way, we are actually saying we want to follow *Love's* way.

The Holy Spirit is the continuing inspiring presence of *Love*.

Evil is the absence or enemy of *Love*.

Forgiveness is the resurgence of *Love*.

Sin is the force against *Love*.

Hate is the rejection of *Love*.

Healing is the regrowth of *Love*.

Prayer is approaching, listening for, and hearing *Love*.

Evangelism is inviting people (those in and out of the church, and those who have rejected it or ignored it) to come join with us (whether they join an institutional church or not) to discover all the ways we and they can live the life of *Love* and give it away, and experience joy at the same time. This is what I believe it means to take seriously the phrase "God *is* Love." This book is about how we have lost the vision that God and Love are literally one and the same.

Love, Then God

This book is also about how, in discovering God as Love, *Love comes first*. Love always precedes our understanding of it, our personification of it, how we explain and present it. Love is what we knew before we knew about God. The traditional approach to explaining Christian ideas, especially to people who are new to its language, is that first we need to understand God, who or what God is, and all God's names—Lord, Creator, Father, Sustainer, Judge, Savior, and so on. Then we need to understand what God has done, who Jesus was and is, what the cross means, what atonement is, what or who the Holy Spirit is, what the Trinity is, and on and on. Finally, once we get all that straight, we learn what we are to do: we are to be obedient to God, to praise God, to Love and follow Jesus, go to church every Sunday (well, most of them . . .), and, as if somehow tacked on at last, oh yes, I almost forgot, we are to Love our neighbors.

As much as my growing-up years in church were designed to teach me about Christian ideas, the one thing that was drilled into me every week was, "God is Love." It was not my understanding of its doctrinal structure that drew me into the Christian faith. I have come to understand that it was, rather, the Love that I had already experienced in my life that brought me here; and it is my ongoing experience of Love, not theological structures, that keeps me here.

It was years and years before I began to put together all the ideas and concepts that form Christian theology (and there are still some I'm not sure I can help you with), but Love was there all the time, right from the start. Sometimes Love was hard to understand and seemed unfair, sometimes painful, and sometimes invisible, such that I thought it absent.

But Love was always there, powerful, fragile, mysterious, constant, visible, and invisible. Love is primary; it comes first, before anything else. The church's faith statements, creeds, systems, stories, narratives, historical reflections, hymns, and all the rest are the words the Spirit has lifted up in the church, words fashioned to express its understanding of things beyond human understanding, and to convey and embody its joyful wonder of the presence of Love in the world. If it helps you to insert the word "God" in that last phrase for "Love," feel free; they are one and the same. But remember, before any of us knew anything about the word "God," or any of those other words, we knew about—and sometimes knew firsthand—Love.

In the pages that follow, I want to suggest the supreme vitality and power of Love in human experience. I want to explore ways we can embrace the vision that God is Love itself, and that of the two, in our life together, we experience Love first. Then, I will suggest ways we can understand what this Love can look like when it comes *first* in the church, the Bible, the Christian story, and the church's life and ministry, along with what I hope will be some simple, comprehensible, comfortable language the church can use to explain itself.

God is Love, but most of the time it is Love that leads us to God rather than the other way around. The problem is that when we do start with Love, Loving-kindness, forgiveness, justice, sacrificial giving, and the rest, and then finally get to the "God" part, the *name* of Love, we leave the uncomplicated "Love" part behind. We start spending more time on theology, what God is like (separating it from what *Love* is like), how Jesus is God's son, the Trinity, creation, the Ten Commandments, Pentecost, Atonement, building up the church, and all the rest.

But primarily we don't need to get people into an organizational or institutional structure or a complex system of belief or doctrine. We need to give the world a song and a chance to sing it. And I know a good one!

3

What Christianity Isn't

Let's get this out of the way

A FATHER AND HIS son are deep in a recurring argument, as the father is fixing supper. The son didn't come home at all last night, out partying until dawn. He was recently graduated from high school, and since he doesn't want to go to college, his father wants him to get a job, pay some of the costs of living at home, and follow the rules of the house about coming home on time. The son wants to live at home and take a year or so off, coming and going as he pleases. More volume. More anger. Shouting. Finally the son screams at his father, "I hate you! You're a terrible father! I don't want to have anything to do with you ever again! I never want to see you again!"

He storms up to his room, slams the door and locks it. Suddenly a grease fire erupts in the skillet on the stove, igniting the curtains at the window. In moments, the kitchen is filled with flames, and the father is unable to stop it. Dark smoke quickly fills the house. The father runs up the stairs and grabs his two younger children, and guides them through the smoke and out of the house to safety.

"What about our brother?" ask the children.

The father looks up at the burning house now totally enveloped in flames. "Your brother has made his choice," he says.

Does your idea of God resemble the father in this disturbing story? In fact, for many people it's a match. In its 2008 study, the Pew Forum on Religion and Public Life reported that 74 percent of Americans believe that if one lives a good life a heavenly reward awaits, while 57 percent believe in hell as a place of torment you go to if you *don't* live a good life, honor God, and have faith.[1]

The general belief of most people seems to be that if you follow God's ways—if you follow the rules and behave, do the right thing, Love your neighbor, don't steal or kill, are not sexually promiscuous, or are not guilty of other offences—then God will accept you and Love you and you will go to heaven when you die. But if you reject God, if you refuse or otherwise fail to live according to the way of Jesus, then you will be eternally lost, or burn in the fire of hell for eternity.

But *that* isn't Christianity!

Or this: The Love of God is free, and God Loves everyone, and you can't buy God's Love with good works, and yet still in the end you will be judged on the good you do or do not do in order for God to decide whether or not you will end up in heaven after you die.

That isn't Christianity either!

Or this: God's Love and salvation are indeed free gifts; you can't do anything to get them or earn them. But you do have to choose to affirm Jesus is God's Son and Lord and Savior in order to get the "free" gift of God's saving Love. Once you do that, you're safe. Those who don't will wish they had, but it will be too late.

Even *that* isn't Christianity!

Confused? Generally, Christian groups affirm that Jesus came to save us from our sins. And yet sin is still all around us and infects our lives, even those who are the most saintly, the most loving, and the most faithful. As one young woman, beaten repeatedly

---

1. Ibid., 10.

by her husband, expressed to me once, "Jesus came to free us from sin, but it must not have worked."

For many seekers and skeptics who are trying to understand the Christian faith, and for those Christians whose faith is fading, the questions raised here are important, hard, and relentless. The answers given by Christians are often complicated and involve deep, lengthy theological concepts that are not easily understood. Often they include glib and practiced "churchy" phrases that seem designed to cut off further discussion rather than encourage it, such as, "Well, you just have to have faith" or "You just have to believe."

Are you beginning to see the problem?

The result has been a growing apathy toward Christianity, the church, and serious questioning and resistance directed toward its message and its invitation. To many, Christianity simply doesn't make sense; it isn't credible, it's complicated, it doesn't engage, and it doesn't excite.

This becomes sadly apparent in the decline of the Christian church in American culture today. The Pew Research Center reports that although 92 percent of Americans affirm certain or fairly certain belief in God,[2] and 78 percent of Americans are at least nominally Christian,[3] only 64 percent of those who claim religious church affiliation consider their faith as "very important," and only 42 percent of Americans who claim some religious affiliation attend services or activities of some kind weekly.[4]

In the meantime, despite a few religious groups holding steady, the "non-affiliated" segment of the American population has been growing much more rapidly than any other demographic group. That number is approaching 70 million persons, fully 20 percent of the American adult population, and 33 percent of adults under 30. There is a popular belief that these persons are spiritually

2. Ibid., 26.

3. Pew, "U.S. Religious Landscape Survey: Religious Affiliation," Executive Summary.

4. Pew, "U.S. Religious Landscape Survey: Religious Beliefs and Practices," 36.

active in their beliefs but they just don't like the church. But only 16 percent of the unaffiliated indicate that religion (their personal spiritual life or something else) is "very important," and nearly 60 percent say it is not important at all. Of all the unaffiliated, 88 percent are not interested in finding a new religion of any kind.[5]

The Pew Research Center has uncovered a number of reasons for persons leaving a congregation and becoming unaffiliated with any religious body, including a sense that churches are more interested in their rules and procedures than the spiritual support of members, there is too much hypocrisy, and there is too much attention paid to power and money, rather than the needs of people. But the two primary reasons that half of all Americans have changed or left religious affiliations at least once in their life are clear. Either they *just drifted away*, or they *simply did not believe in God or the teachings of the faith group*. Apparently the lines that connected them to the church came undone, and perhaps without anyone noticing they slipped away and were gone.[6] The primary reason for this appears to be that *the teaching about God and the rest of the faith system was not clear or exciting or inspiring enough to hold that line tight*. It is obvious that the Christian church in the U.S. is undergoing serious decline. Churches *are* trying to reach out to new disciples. But according to the statistics, it doesn't seem to be very effective.

I indicated above that I believe that part of the problem is the language and translation problem: that because of the onslaught of scientific technical development in human experience, we are speaking a different language than those we are trying to reach. I fervently hope that the church can reorient its language to be more sensitive to the presence of the Spirit among us, and affirm Love, unselfish giving, and caring as the central definition of what the Christian faith is and what the church is about. But even if we do there is still a deeper problem, and a danger to be avoided. The way the church and the churches have always communicated their

5. Pew, "'Nones' on the Rise" Executive Summary.
6. Pew, "Faith in Flux," Executive Summary.

experiences and conclusions about God and Christianity with the world is with a "message," "news," a body of information. If people were just in possession of this information, or system, or language, it could change their lives. So we tell them.

But whatever the church attempts to *tell* people, whether it is from the Bible or a theological system, or a sermon, or even an experience, it is received—in a scientific, technical culture—as intellectual content to engage the mind. It is assumed (or hoped) that people will read it or listen to it, evaluate it intelligently, and be convinced ("convicted" is the word sometimes used) that it is right, good, reasonable, and true. When they fully understand it, they will agree to "follow" Jesus by joining a church. It is often assumed that when this happens then the work of the church is done. The system worked.

However, the Love that is the essence of the Christian faith cannot be fully assimilated as part of intellectual information, or as an organized system. I don't mean to denigrate theological writings or structures. They can be helpful in identifying and conceptualizing what is really important in any religious system. They can assist us get our thoughts in clear order, so that we don't say things we don't mean. They can be intensely satisfying, even inspiring. But this Love which is God present comes first, before the theological systems that attempt to explain it. It is the energy and substance that informs any system. It is what theological systems are supposed to be about. It is prior to the careful explanations of Christianity about life in the world. Theological systems can give us words to use in talking *about* God, and *about* Love. But Love as the essence of the Christian faith cannot simply be a bigger add-on to the current theological language or a larger more prominent rewrite in the creeds or the system. Our current way of talking about the Christian faith must be renewed and reformed. We must enable the primacy of active Love, God present, to work its way into our entire church life, if we wish our story to be clearly understood. We must sharpen the focus of what we mean by the life of Love, rather than allow it to appear simply as a projected outcome of correct, organized belief.

Even if the language of Love is clarified in the church's theological system, and pervasive in the life of the church similar to the way I will describe in the pages that follow, the danger still exists that it could still be communicated only as information, and will not reach those who need it most. Love, God present, cannot be fully communicated in a written word or system. It can only be communicated in the living of it. *Being Christian is not what you think. It's what you do.* Depending on spreading Love through a booklet or a lecture or a system to be taught or an expert to be interviewed leads to confusion, resistance, misunderstanding, rejection, or, most likely, a complete lack of interest. Furthermore, my experience as a pastor tells me that a significant number of churchgoing people have the same concerns and confusions about the contents of theological systems and writings they are apparently supposed to embrace. They may come to church because of family connections, or out of habit, or because it's good for the children, or it's good for business, or it's a nice group of friends with the same values. If asked in polls if they believe in God, I suspect that many of them answer in the affirmative because it is quite uncomfortable and unacceptable to publically, or even privately, answer any other way. Secretly mystified, not wanting to be out of step with the rest, they have never really questioned what everyone else seems to understand and readily accept.

A farmer told me he was turned off by his understanding that one of the requirements to be a good Christian is to intellectually affirm ("have faith") that something written in a book (the Bible) long ago in a prescientific age is true, when it goes totally against his scientific understanding of the world. Why, he asked, should a religious assertion about a Loving God be presented as an anti-scientific hurdle to jump over? Why should trusting God require suspending a cognitive understanding of the beautifully complex world God made, and the refusal to use the minds God gave us? Why couldn't truth simply be truth?

A young garage mechanic said he could not affirm the Bible as the true and authoritative Word of God when the only evidence of that was that the Bible *said* it was, or that the pastor said it was, or that Mom or Dad said it was.

A middle-age doctor wrote that a minister told him that Jesus sacrificially died to pay the price of his sin, to which he responded that, in the first place, he didn't believe in the efficacy of human sacrifice of any kind, and that it was wrong, and furthermore, what kind of Being or Power demanded to be paid off by the death of his son? If God was going to save me, why didn't he just go ahead and do it, instead of going through all this payoff stuff? Is this some kind of rule or regulation that God is required to follow? If so, who set *that* up? And furthermore, if he paid off my sin, why am I still sinning, and why is sin still all around me? If he died for me, in my place, then why am I still going to die?

A Silicon Valley engineer-turned-soccer-mom said that when she was a child her pastor told her that if she would just say and believe that Jesus is the Son of God, she would go to heaven when she dies. Otherwise, she would go to hell. She never went back, explaining that she couldn't just *decide* to believe something like that anymore than she could just decide to believe that green was red, and that furthermore she would have nothing to do with such a hateful God. Anyhow, she said, the whole thing seemed like a very selfish, self-centered religion, organized for self-preservation; people willing to do anything they had to do, affirm anything they had to affirm, say anything they had to say in order to get themselves to heaven when they died, and to hell (literally) with everybody else, no matter how good or unselfish or loving they were. This desire to save themselves at any cost seemed to her an appeal to the lowest, basest, and most selfish of all human motivations. It was fundamentally immoral, and made no sense. She knew some church people, she said, and what they were like outside church. Many of their lives did not match what she heard them say in church, and she decided she didn't want to be a part of it.

These are from real conversations—you can't make this stuff up—and are hard words to hear. Churches have tried to respond in a variety of ways. Some churches contend that if you don't understand these things, don't worry about it; just be filled with the Spirit, for that emotional experience is more important than intellectual understanding of the faith. Other churches, seeking intellectual understanding, redouble their efforts to clarify their theological systems, parts of which, when found to be unbelievable by the mind, are presented as "unknowable," or "best left to God," or as subject matter for "faith."

Some churches, perhaps realizing that people may never fully understand complex theological systems enough to fully embrace them (having noticed how unenthusiastically they mutter their prayers and creedal statements in Sunday worship), rely on fun, entertaining, hip and happy worship (with the sad loss, in my opinion, of a sense of awe and humility before the majesty of God in worship) to get new members. They have found that people respond to gyms, health-club-type activities, dinners, clubs, golf tournaments, family activities systems, professional childcare, or schools that require church membership. Even churches for whom emotion is a central part of worship and church life, who may not wrestle so much with the systematic problems of theological doctrines and ideas, often structure into their life the same kinds of elements designed to attract people to a large and therefore "successful" institutional operation.

These kinds of community-building activities are not necessarily wrong. They may serve as a way to foster and encourage experiences of Love in all its faces. But unless understood and presented and formed that way, and unless the connection is made that they are what the Christian faith is all about, they will more likely be perceived as just more consumer goods to be purchased, or as the cost of doing business for a successful institution. The drive for a successful institution becomes the substance of the message of the church to the community, which is the wrong message and *not what Christianity is*. Churches that offer a large variety of such activities often indicate that they are meant to get people into the church, where they can then hear the gospel message, but such activities also indicate the possibility that the gospel message as presented is not strong enough on its own to excite people to be a part of the church, the body of Love, the Body of Christ.

What is needed is a full re-examination of how we present the Christian faith, beyond written words, sermons, documents, theological systems, and even beyond our story. *These structured words alone will not do.* What is needed is a rediscovery of the clear and uncomplicated truth of the faith that was originally born out of experiences of the heart, experiences of Love itself, the one who walked among us and walks among us still, experiences that still speak primarily to the heart. These kinds of experiences will then yield theological reflections that are easily and quickly understood and accepted by the discipline of the twenty-first-century mind, and can be shared and communicated in a clear, uncluttered, accessible, credible simplicity.

I don't believe that the problem in truly reaching people, both religious and non-religious, in the depths of their souls is one of worship style or marketing or music or type of building or time or place. I believe it is a problem of theology that relies on information and systems and structure, rather than a church defining itself, and presenting itself, simply as living a life of Love. The faith as triumphant and universal Love, when it is experienced and joyfully embraced first in the heart, lends itself to a simple explanation that is fully and easily acceptable in the thoughtful mind. The point is that reflecting theologically on this kind of experience of the Holy has no battle with science or worldviews. It is able to be understood as a faith that is just as exciting to persons with a twenty-first-century worldview as it was to persons with a first-century worldview, a faith that is not dependent on either and transcends both.

When Jesus spoke to the people of Judea and the surrounding countryside during the years of his itinerant ministry, what he said *made sense* to them. They quickly understood it because they could see and experience firsthand the Love that he lived. Their worldview was not scientific in our sense of the word. They were not concerned with the "science" of what Jesus did. When he healed someone or brought about what we might call a supernatural act, they did not ask, "How did you do that?" as we would. They asked instead, "What does this mean?"[7] The science of it, how it happened, wasn't the point. It was simply a context. The point was the healing, the Loving touch of Jesus.

The New Testament writers had the same understanding of the world. Their reporting is sometimes quite mysterious to us if we allow the assumptions of their writings about how the world works to eclipse the centrality of their presentation of who Jesus is and was: the human face of God, the human face of Love. Jesus touched them (just as he can and does touch us) in their hearts. It was startling and challenging in many ways, but it was not confusing and it made sense to them in the world in which they lived. It was immediately exciting and they yearned to be a part of it. Otherwise, people would not have kept coming to see him and hear him in such numbers as are reported in the Gospels. They didn't require doctrinal study groups, theological diagrams, lectures, and theological libraries filled with thick multivolume systematic theologies to figure it all out. He was speaking to them in their own language, in their own stories, in their own culture, in their own world, and in words and word pictures and Old Testament concepts they recognized without need of interpretation. It was enough for them. There was an immediate personal link, and whether they accepted him or rejected him, there was hardly any question as to what he was saying. Although they did not fully understand him until after the cross and resurrection, he touched and ignited their hearts, long before they understood him with their minds. He was the face of God's Love, not the face of God's systematic theology.

I am convinced, from my conversations with many who have little interest in religion of any kind, that they, like those Jesus touched, do in fact yearn for a truly deep, solid, life challenging, spiritual, even emotional engagement with a reliable anchor in their lives. But it needs to be one that does not do violence to their understanding of the world in which they live, and is both credible and simple. It must appeal to their better angels rather than

7. For example, see Mark 1:27 and Acts 2:14.

what they perceive in the church—rightly or wrongly—as selfish and manipulative. They want to cut through all the dogma and the doctrines and the creeds and the emotion, to find a simple, uncomplicated, unvarnished truth that truly *excites* them. Although many of them profess a belief in some kind in God, they simply do not perceive that the Christian faith makes sense to them today. It does not touch them in their minds or in their hearts in the way Jesus touched his hearers in the first century. Many persons who are unaffiliated and uninterested believe that being Christian, being in the church, means giving intellectual assent to propositions (creation in six days, virgin birth, the Trinity, resurrection, heaven, hell, miracles, atonement theories—for example, the efficacy of human sacrifice—and so on) that they cannot believe, or joining in emotional gymnastics they do not feel. They don't understand the complexities of the Christian faith and theological doctrines, they don't feel it, and they aren't buying it. It's just too much trouble. For the most part, they aren't arguing about it and they aren't attacking it; they are just leaving it alone.

But Christianity is not about a God who is lying in wait for people to do something wrong or to screw something up, in order to punish or destroy them.

Christianity is not a systematic theology or a body of statements of fact or propositions or stories that people must learn and affirm as true.

Christianity is not about a God who can be bribed, paid off with crucifixions, money, right belief, or good behavior so that people can get what they want.

Christianity is not a resource to make people carefree and protected from the pain and sorrow and injustice of the world.

Christianity is not about somehow getting more people in church than last week, or more than the church down the street, thus becoming a successful institution.

Christianity is not a system by which you can be assured that your enemies and those you don't like will be punished.

Christianity is not a hiding place to avoid the challenges of the world and the needs of its people for kindness, forgiveness, care, justice, food, clothing, a place to live, and the experience of joy.

Christianity is not a system that has as its goal getting people safely into heaven when they die.

So then what is it? Well, you can tell where this is going. You already know. I suggest a different, uncomplicated way to understand the Christian faith. I suggest that what is needed is a fully simplified reorientation of our understanding of the faith, so that when it is presented to the world, the immediate "aha"-moment response is, "Oh! Of course! It's obvious! It was there all the time! I see! I can do that! I *want* to do that!"

I suggest that we need to understand that God is Love, and that Love is the core of our faith—receiving it, giving it away, healed and renewed by it, celebrating it, living it in every corner of our lives. The rest, with various levels of importance, is secondary.

4

What Christianity Is

Being Christian isn't what you
think, it's what you do

Whoever does not Love does not
know God, for God is Love.[1]

IT IS A WARM spring-green West Virginia afternoon and I am
knocking on the door of a small, unimposing home where a couple
in our church has lived together since their marriage sixty-four
years ago. This is the eve of their anniversary and their children are
coming from out of town to take them to dinner tomorrow. They
are both eighty-five years old, and they share an occasional smile
as they tell me about their lives. There is something special about
these two people for whom the fullness of years has worn down
all the rough edges, and left them with a treasury of memories
encased in just that smile. They had grown up in the same village. He worked in the hardware store, and she said she made lots
of visits there and had about run out of things to buy, reasons to
come, when one day he finally asked her to take a walk with him.
She said, "We waded around in the shallow water for a long time,
and then that old river Love just swept us away."

1. 1 John 4:8.

The surprisingly uncomplicated truth and substance of the Christian faith, in its simplest form, is this: people gathered together by the power of the Spirit to live a particular way of life, the life of active, unselfish, and life-enriching Love. Their singular intention is to orient life around unconditional, sacrificial Love, and to extend kindness, forgiveness, justice, fairness, and joy into every life and circumstance everywhere.

Stripped of its complexities, Christianity's bottom line is this:

Love your neighbor.

It is people swept away by that old river Love.

It is not a collection of elaborate doctrines, dogmas, and beliefs that you have to learn and affirm or stories that you must believe, some of which defy the rational thinking mind. Neither is it about a God who is out to get you if you don't behave or believe correctly.

Christianity is not just some kind of weekly cheering squad or pep rally to get people up and excited or ecstatic for God that only exists on Sunday morning. The essence of Christianity is simply people gathered together who affirm, celebrate, live, and give away the gift of Love. *Being Christian is not what you think* or some kind of theological system you affirm intellectually; it is not your ideas *about* God, or Jesus, or creation, or atonement, or the Trinity, or the Bible. You may freely believe that Jesus was just a spellbinding travelling salesman, or a political revolutionary out to undermine the Roman government, or a six-foot-five weight lifter who carried a King James Bible with him, or the world's first hippie. There is plenty of room in this boat for all kinds of viewpoints, and we can be enriched by each other and our differences.

Being Christian is not what you *think is true*; it is *what you do*. Being Christian is the decision, the intentional will, to Love your neighbor, putting Love into practice and investing in Loving-kindness. It is celebrating universal, forgiving, never-ceasing Love, and figuring out new ways to give it away. Being Christian is joining together to share the experience of the powerful, creative presence of

Love in all the world for the enrichment of every life on the planet. It is the Love that surges through creation like a mighty river.

Christianity is Love that is made visible. It is Love put into practice. It has always been there all around you. It will always be there. It is there now, waiting to be discovered and enacted.

In the 1960s, before the Berlin wall came down, an American visitor boarded a train that took him from the West Berlin into East Berlin, behind the wall, on a one-day permit. He met at length with the editor of a Christian magazine and learned about life there, then walked through the city, had a meal, and even attended an outdoor orchestral concert in a park. As it began to get dark, he made his way back to the train station, only to discover that he didn't have enough money left to buy a ticket back to the West. There was only one other person in the station, standing behind him in line. As he hesitated, wondering what he would do, the man reached around him and put coins and bills down on the metal counter to buy the ticket. They sat together on the nearly empty train, and although they could find no common language they managed to converse through signs, photographs, and broken words, and in a very short time became friends. At the last station in the East, the two men stood and took each other's hand, knowing they would probably not meet again. The East German got off the train, and the American went on safely back to the West.

The summer after his high school graduation, a young man came to the little New Hampshire town to live with his grandparents while attending a nearby community college. It was the late 1960s, and they couldn't understand or tolerate his long hair, teenage dress style, or the wild music he loved. They were approaching their eighties and lived by a different code of how life should be lived. He and they were unable to connect with each other. Whole nights spent out, drugs, alcohol, and run-ins with the police made it unbearable. Later, in a successful rock band, magazines and books quoted his hate-filled rejection of them and what he then considered their useless lives and outdated values, and how he despised being with them (words he regretted in later life). They could not avoid what he said about them, but his grandmother, who attended a famous Eastern music conservatory in her youth and played and loved classical music all her life, went out and bought a little transistor radio so she could carry it with her and listen to rock stations in order to hear him and his music. It didn't matter what he had said about her; he was her grandson, and she Loved him, and she never stopped Loving him.

A social worker always took her little girls with her to nursing homes when she had work to do there, because she wanted them to learn the beauty and worth of older persons. One day, her eight-year-old struck up a conversation with an elderly woman in a wheelchair in a hallway, while her mother engaged in her work elsewhere. They made their way through the hallways, laughed with each other, and told stories to each other about their lives and experiences, and when it was time to go they hugged each other with promises to return, which were later fulfilled. "I Love you," said the little girl. "I Love you too," said the woman. As they were leaving, the little girl looked up at her mother and said, "I think I made her day." "She made yours too," thought her mother. All the while the elderly woman was telling her friends the same thing.

Two men only knew each other slightly when they became deacons in their church. They confided to each other that they were glad to have been chosen, but were very uneasy about the part of the training about ministering to people in need, which was their main function as deacons. One worked for a delivery service and the other was a teacher, but neither was too excited about learning how to be a caregiver. They were assigned to a pleasant elderly woman who needed a ride to church, and they thought that shouldn't be too demanding. As the months went by, they either went together with their families to pick her up or alternated weeks. They began to take her to other church activities and to some school programs with their children. She became almost a member of their families, and her homemade cookies became legendary. She had a slight stroke and they stayed with her in the emergency room. It was late and she still hadn't been admitted, and they sat with her and held her hand, and she cried a little and said she was afraid. They stayed until she was safely in a room, just after 2:30 a.m., and in the days to come they were there every day to see her. They and their families helped her recover at home with constant visits and care. It was only a few years until, stopping to get her for church one Sunday morning and hearing no answer at the door, they found that she had died during the night. "Knowing her and caring for her, helping her out," they agreed, "was like a massive infusion of Love into our lives and our families' lives. It made different people out of us."

The university class was just underway when cries and sounds of running feet exploded in the hallway. A sound that could only be gunfire filled the air. They crowded to the door to see, and sure enough, there he was, firing into the classrooms and at anyone still unhidden. He moved down the hallway, jerking open a door and shooting at random. The professor slammed the classroom door shut. There was no lock. "Quick, out the windows!" he cried. "It's only about a six-foot drop! Do it! Now!" The sound of shooting was deafening. He turned and put his foot up on the frame beside the door and, pulling as hard as he could with both hands, he held the door shut. The shooter pulled from the other side, and pulled again, then fired through it, fired again, and the professor fell to the floor lifeless just as the last student jumped from the window ledge to safety. As he picked himself up, he looked back up at the open window, and suddenly flashed on a line from his childhood, "Greater love than this no one has . . ."

These accounts of Love are true! You can't make this stuff up! Flooding out across the hours of every day, waiting to be seen and lived, is Love, like a great river, sweeping away into itself all who seek—and some who just accidently fall in—its joyful, life-saving, adventurous flow. I know what you're thinking: All this Love stuff sounds like the sixties all over again—flower power, sweetness and light, happy endings, lost puppies found, love bathed in shallow innocence. You probably feel a slight embarrassment at the assertion that something as important as our religious life is based on such a naïve and shallow concept. But this Love is much deeper and more fundamental than simple euphoria, a heart-shaped bumper sticker, or a superficial, sometimes even manufactured happiness.

This is the Love that is sometimes experienced in deep lifelong friendships that have weathered storms and shaking foundations.

Sometimes it is found in an event of great joy that draws thousands of people together in a wonderful shared effort or celebration.

Sometimes it is as silent as sunrise, with the touch of a hand on a shoulder.

Often it is Love that appears undeserved, sometimes only one-sided, extended without conditions or requirements for Love in return.

Sometimes it is Love that is constant, uninterrupted, in the middle of unbearable change and upheaval.

Sometimes it appears in large-scale worldwide efforts to feed hungry refugees, or medical relief for victims of war, epidemic, and illness, or help for those who need housing or clean water or relief from persecution or bigotry.

Often Love is intentional kindness to family and friends, and to those we do not know and will probably never see again.

Sometimes Love works itself out over many years of hard effort, from one generation to another, sometimes over many generations, working with others in righting wrongs, seeking to overcome forces that harm and degrade human life, and striving for a peaceful human community, sometimes in political arenas nationally and internationally. Sometimes it is triggered by hearing a piece of music, or experiencing a painting, or in a scientific discovery, a mathematical formula, an architectural project, a book, an organ transplant, a sunrise, a walk in a West Virginia wood, a view of the stars on a clear moonless mountaintop, or the birth of a baby.

Sometimes it appears in forgiveness, a healing reconciliation with no need for winners or losers.

Sometimes it appears in surrounding support when there is tragedy, sudden pain, even death.

Sometimes Love apparently fails, disappears from view, and, as far as we can see, does not seem to find its way into the lives of persons suffering from depression or other illness, or those whose lives are centered only on themselves and the accumulation of power, and who inflict pain without remorse.

But even when it is unseen, Love is there, and it will always find its way. It is the primary motivation behind the struggle for justice for people and nations, the desire to make things right in a world filled with greed and a striving for selfish power.

Love seems most clear when it is the result of unselfish sacrifice, when you have to give something up to be a part of its creation where there is overwhelming need.

All persons everywhere who embrace the unique singular power of Love as unequaled in all experience—all who know or have known it or yearn for it, all who affirm it as life's most important element, all who want to give it away where it is needed most—are already at one with Christianity.

This is what Christianity is. Embracing Love is embracing God. It's just that simple.

Love is more basic and primary in our religious lives than we often imagine. Suppose that during the first half of the twentieth century there was a manufacturing company that made typewriters and supporting materials like carbon paper, typewriter stands, chairs, lights, and all manner of paper, business supplies, and equipment. But typewriters were the company's big profit item, and its primary product. Life was good, business was booming, and the company was considering getting into the printing business, letterhead design, advertising materials, and who knew what else. Before taking a step that big, a planning conference was held, led by an outside business consultant, to explore what this new addition would look like and how it fit into the future of the company. The consultant asked what he called the central question, "What business are you actually in?" Most participants believed that they were in the typewriter business or in the business of producing office machinery of various kinds. But after hours of searching conversation, it turned out they discovered they were actually in the information business: they were providing equipment and supplies so that people and businesses could easily and economically communicate ideas and information with each other. This realization enabled them to focus on a successful future development oriented around methods of communication and managing and transmitting information, rather than just building typewriters (which today are almost extinct). They acted just in time for the computer revolution.

The same story could apply to the coal business in my own state of West Virginia. Many coal company owners believe they are in the coal business, but it seems to me that they are actually in the energy business, supplying the materials needed for its production and use. As coal reserves are used up, they might need to concentrate on other forms of energy, such as solar, water, wind, geothermal, fusion, and others, for the good of their company and its employees.

I think the church can learn something here. Please forgive me for the crassness of my language (it goes against the grain), but here goes: we in the church are convinced that we are in the "God business." We want to take God to the nations and sing God's praises. We want to bring people to Jesus and we want them to follow him. We want people to experience the Holy Spirit. Our church life and especially our worship are centered on God and

Jesus and the Holy Spirit in prayers and hymns and sermons, creedal statements, and other elements of the liturgy. We spend much of our time talking about, praying to, praising, singing about, studying, examining, and trying to understand God, the life and death and resurrection of Jesus, and the presence of the Spirit. Any systematic writing about theology and what the church is all about typically begins with God, and then goes from there—what God is like, where God is, how we can please God, what the relationship is between God and Jesus and the Holy Spirit and the church, whether God changes his mind, whether God really Loves homosexuals, ex-prisoners, or Muslims, and why God only answer certain prayers and not others. When we (in the Presbyterian Church anyway) ordain ministers and elders, we ask what they believe to be true facts about the faith, what their religious beliefs are about God. We are supposed to tell people about God and to convince people to follow Christ. This is the "business" we're in.

But behind all this is the business we are *really* in—what God is trying to tell us to *do* and the kind of people God is telling us to *be*. Sometimes we get so enamored with what God is like, so focused on figuring out what Jesus really said or what the Spirit is like, that we lose sight of what they are trying to tell us to *do*, who they want us to *be*, the gift that they have for us. It seems to me that we are just missing the whole point.

Several times I have tried to teach my dog Frisco, who is smart enough, but certainly not offensively so, to bring a ball back to me when I throw it. "There it is, Frisco baby, go get it! It's over there, go get it!" But she was so interested in me and my enthusiasm and the finger I was pointing at the ball (possibly because I had a treat in there somewhere to entice and reward her) that she totally ignored what I was pointing at. *She knew where the goodies were.*

Sometimes we see so many potential treats, possible rewards, or interesting sights when God speaks to us and when we talk about God that we overlook entirely what God is trying to tell us. We overlook what God is pointing at, where God wants us to go, what God wants us to do. What God is pointing at, the whole point of the Christian faith, is the presence of Love in creation, what it looks like, and how it transforms human life. What God wants us to do is to discover what that Love is like, to make Love the guiding principle and motivation in our lives, and to give Love away.

But we know where the goodies are, and we spend an inordinate amount of time talking about what God is like, what the Trinity is, how Jesus figures in, how to please God, how to accept Jesus, and how to pray correctly in order to get what we want. We sing hymns to God, draw pictures of God, tell God what a wonderful God he is, and here's what we want him to do. And all the while God is pointing to Love and Loving-kindness, care, and forgiveness. God is saying to us, "It's over there! What you're looking for is over there! Go get it, use it; it's not really yours until you give it away. There it is, it's free, over there!"

The whole Christian story, from creation to incarnation to resurrection, is simply a *revelation,* an uncovering of the Love with which God has filled up this world. Love has been there from the beginning of creation. God isn't making it up as the years go by. God got it right the first time. The gift of Love is the most important thing in all creation.

We are indeed in the "God business." It is *God* we want to take to the nations.

It is *Jesus* to whom we want to bring people.

It is the power of the *Spirit* we want people to experience.

But this "business," said differently and perhaps more clearly to this struggling world, is simply this:

It is *Love* as a way of life we want to take to the nations.

It is *Loving-kindness, compassion, and justice* to which we want to bring people.

It is *forgiving, universal, joyful Love* we want people to discover and experience.

It is not correct dogma, not emotion, not "success," not even good behavior that transforms life. Only Love can do that. For when we experience Love, we experience God. Love is what God is.

The essence of Christianity is not primarily what we think or believe is true *about* God or Jesus or the Holy Spirit. It is not about how we think the universe is structured or how it works, about church doctrines, the Bible, how much we talk about them, argue about them, or celebrate them. All that is certainly helpful, and careful unhurried hours studying theology and the Bible lead to deeper understanding of how Love unfolds.

But Christianity is about what is *behind* these ideas and systems, from which they spring and to which they point. Love, as the essence of the joyful life, is the reason for the development of theological ideas and doctrines, it is the truth they carry, it is the substance of what they explain and describe. Love is what theological systems want us to know, firsthand. The religious life, the Christian life, is about the discovery of Love and the life oriented around Love. It is not so important that we understand everything *about* God or how God works or doesn't work, or what God looks like, or whether God has weight or mass. It is not so important that we understand everything *about* Jesus, that we figure out how Jesus' miracles worked, or how he did them, or his precise words, or where he lived, or whether or not he had a girlfriend. It is not so important that we understand everything *about* the Bible or that we try to recreate our cultural norms to match everything in it, or have a Bible verse to back up everything we think or do.

What is important is that we *know* God, that we *know* Jesus, by engaging intentionally in the life of Love, that we purposefully extend unconditional, universal Love beyond ourselves, and orient our lives around Loving-kindness and care and justice, for that is who and where God is. What is important is that we reach out to the world around us with forgiving, healing, sacrificial Love. It is in the experience of extending of Love beyond ourselves that we find the true depth and power and deepest joy of life and of the Holy, for when we embrace Love, we embrace God.

Try this: every time you come across the words "God," "Jesus," and "Holy Spirit" in the Bible, substitute the word "Love" there. You might be surprised at what you find. God *is* Love. Christians embrace Love as they embrace God as the central, most influential, most powerful element in all of human experience.

We don't create this Love. It comes to us as a free gift, "delivered" to us to be delivered beyond ourselves, freely given so that it can be given away, designed to be spread. We take no credit for it. It's a part of us from beyond ourselves. We don't Love in order to be Loved back, or to possess joy or anything else, as if we were somehow living the life of Love in order to be rewarded. When we engage in compassion or forgiveness or sacrificial Love, there is no striving for a reward, but there is a rewarding simultaneous result. The result, the joyful experience of a Loving God, is experienced *at the moment the Love is being given.* This is the Love that will not let us go.

Once upon a time (any time will do) there was a town at the edge of a great ocean that found itself cut off from the rest of the world (I don't remember why—blizzards or landslides or an epidemic of some kind). No one could get in or out, planes and trains were unable to function, and roads were out. Supplies were dwindling fast. Medicine, clothing, food, and water were all in short supply. People were frustrated, weary, and angry. One particularly dark and overcast day, when the townspeople had just about given up hope, a ship unexpectedly appeared in the harbor. Cranes began unloading huge crates filled with everything the people needed—warm clothing, nourishing food, water, medicine, even toys for the children. It was a gift from a philanthropist who had helped settle the town years before and who heard of its distress. The gifts, he said, were given only because this was his town too, he Loved the townspeople, and they were in need of help. More ships arrived every day, and soon the dock was covered by stacks and stacks of these countless gifts of Love. The philanthropist's representative arrived to show the population how the gifts were to be given. They were to be faithfully distributed by a group of people who would call themselves "servers" (okay, "Christians," but let's not get ahead of ourselves; work with me here) and would work together with many, many others. As they gave the gifts away, it became for them an experience of *receiving* a gift, *receiving* Love, and as Love flowed through the town, those who received the gifts became servers themselves. All were drawn to the provider of the gifts, in gratitude for the gifts and for his great Love for them and their town. They gathered together and expressed their thanks to him, and sang songs of thanksgiving, and examined, talked about, and reflected on his benevolence to them. But he pointed them in another direction, for their primary life-giving task was not to stay in their buildings and talk about him and come up with all kinds of new ways to thank him for his gifts; rather it was *to unpack those crates waiting on the docks, to share and deliver the goods*, to celebrate the Love in those crates, and give it all away. The gifts were for everyone who needed them, not just those who could pay, or who had the right contacts, or had the right "beliefs," or who had been good enough, or who spoke well of the giver, or even knew who the giver was. These gifts injected Love into the town, the way it was when it first began (otherwise referred to as "the good old days"). They contained not only food and medicine; every gift was filled with a generous supply of Love and care, kindness and support, forgiveness and encouragement, which mystically spilled from each box as it was opened, out like a vapor into the air, and flowed into the lives of the weary inhabitants like a gentle summer rain at the end of a hot day. Frustration, weariness, and anger began to subside. Every time a box was opened, someone was suddenly enabled to Love, to understand what it was like to be Loved, and to recognize and spread Love. These gifts were not just the evidence of Love. They were Love itself.

Just so, God has freely placed the Spirit of Love, as a living force among our whole human family, waiting to be opened and uncovered and embraced and distributed.

Christianity is not just believing that certain things are true and others are not. Nor is it only a prescribed emotional experience, feeling a certain way and not feeling another way. Christianity at its core is simply discovering and intentionally, purposefully extending beyond yourself the gift of life-giving Love, for Love is never really yours until you give it away. Being comforted and strengthened by it, finding the new life it holds for you, comes from giving it away freely, establishing it where it is absent, and celebrating it and the way it transforms human life. Love is the vital spark and the simple truth of the Christian faith. This is Christianity in its simplest, purest form. This is where life's true purpose and joy are waiting to be found.

This is what Christianity is! This is the Love that will not let us go!

My friend, if you believe this simple truth—that Love, Loving, and being Loved is the most important thing in the world, the most powerful and influential element of human experience—and you want to orient your life around it and give it away to someone else, then (whether you use the language of this or that church, or no institutional church at all) you are already one of us. That's all there is to it. It's just that simple. If you get that, you get it all.

5

The Church

And the gathering
of practitioners

MY FIRST WORK AS a pastor was in two small rural churches, one in a small town, my primary responsibility, and another out in the country. It was there, under their guidance, that my education as a minister literally *began*. I was fresh out of school and the people in these churches were my teachers. They were good at it. In the Presbyterian Church, the ruling body, made up of persons elected by the congregation—called elders—is the Session, and the pastor of the church is the chairperson—called the moderator—of the Session. So after a few weeks on the job it occurred to me that maybe we ought to have a meeting of the Session of the church in town. We met that evening in the conference room of the little bank building because, unlike the church, it was air-conditioned. It was the first Session meeting I had ever chaired, and I was nervous about it. There were six elders on the Session. They were very kind and we worked our way successfully through the meeting. Presbyterians like to say we do things "decently and in order," and that's what we did, although somewhat informally. After the meeting, they decided that their new minister should drive over to meet Clark Foster. We all piled into two cars and drove over to a small comfortable looking house on the outskirts of the town. On the way, they explained to me that the church building was built in the 1920s with a mortgage from a bank in Charlotte. Then came the Depression in the 1930s, and it got harder and harder to make the payments. So the members of the church Session, every one of them, in the middle of the Depression, took out second mortgages on their own homes to pay off the mortgage on the church. This was in addition to their regular tithes to the other ministries of the church. They were totally devoted to their church and their God, and they felt it was their duty as church leaders to do what was needed. The elders told me they were children when that happened, but they remembered, and it was an important part of the church's story. Clark Foster was the last living member of that Session. He had amassed many years by that time and was house-bound, but he was warm and gracious, and we all sat in his living room that night and told stories about the church and the town. It was sparkling and it was magical. After awhile, one of the elders led us in prayer and we drove away.

Whenever I think of the whole Christian church in general, I remember that night, for I have never felt the power and the overwhelming Love of the Spirit more than during that evening. They knew what church was. We had just spent time in our meeting about the structure and rules and institutional elements of the church, and afterward we spent time in Clark Foster's living room experiencing what and who the church truly was. I was among practitioners who truly knew what they were doing.

The church is the gathering together of all who have discovered that God and Love are inseparable, and that this *unity* of God and Love is the most important component of our life together.

In much of the history of its theology, the church has expressed one of its primary goals as being the body of Christ, living the life of Jesus, who presented the face of God to the world. Affirming that God is Love, the Love that is God's presence, perhaps a more clear expression of our goal is to be the body of *Love*, to live the life of *Love*, to extend *Love* beyond ourselves. Our purpose is not simply to distribute information to the world. Our purpose is to bring experiences of *Love* and healing joy to those that have never known it and yet yearn for it, those who have forgotten it, or who have lost sight of it and need to be reminded of it, as I was that night in Clark Foster's living room. We can tell people where all that Love comes from later.

The church has a particular stewardship of Love, but not in the sense that only the church has the power to dispense or withhold Love in the world. Although sometimes hidden, Love is already there, already free. The church doesn't have to create it; it is only to be part of the means of its release and its growth. The character of the church's stewardship of Love is more as a servant of Love, a servant who not only implements and extends Love, but points out where in the world Love already exists, where it is waiting to be uncovered, set in motion, celebrated, and shared.

Each person who is a part of the church is, in some way, a practitioner of that Love, a practitioner of God, whether they want to be or not, whether they realize it or not, whether they are actually extending Love or not. In fact, many of us who are in the family of the church are wounded and hurt from time to time by some unloving circumstance in life and are in need of *receiving* Love. But in time we will discover a supreme healing that comes from the Love of the fellowship, and again will become one of the active practitioners of Love.

Practitioners need to understand that sometimes what passes for Love in the world is twisted and unrecognizable. As they sift through life's experiences they need to be diligent in seeking to understand authentic God-Love, what it looks like and how works, and how they can sharpen their skills and insight in order to deal with the world's imperfections. Love is not God-Love when it is selfish, for one's own self-centered satisfaction or advantage. It is not God-Love when it results in painful injury or injustice in any form or when it degrades another. When it is only temporary, when it is contingent on behavior or success, when it is unforgiving or dependent on another's confession or apology, then it is not God-Love. It is not God-Love when it leaves anybody out or when it rises from a sense of hubris or superiority. This twisted love results in persons who do not fully experience the Love that is God's presence, or the joy it brings.

When practitioners carry the face of Love to another, they carry the real actual presence of God. This is the Love that doesn't depend on recognition or being thanked, on anyone ever knowing it even happened, or knowing its results. This is Love given freely for the gift of life. Life in the presence and celebration of Love is how creation is meant to be for all people everywhere. This is what God wants for the whole human family, and all creation. This is how God created life to be.

The church is designed to be an intentional presence (but not the only location) of true God-Love in the world. What is needed is a renewed vision of the Christian church that has moved beyond propagating "right" belief and doctrine, that has moved beyond building up successful institutions, and has moved beyond defining the Christian life as whatever behavior will please God in order to get good things, like a care-free life, good health, success, respect, money, or heaven. We need to dispense with the flawed image in which everybody should be alike, just like "us," and believe the same thing theologically, culturally, philosophically, and every other way—embrace the same ideas, vote the same way, live the same way, and think the same way. The Love that is the presence of God, and that is the main component of the church, is for all kinds of persons, all kinds of backgrounds, colors, sizes, shapes, and DNA, and excludes no one.

But the truth is, to think of the church in terms of uniformity or differences, as if trying to achieve some kind of optimal pattern or desired goal, is a distraction. The substance of a deeper vision of the church, which we celebrate and to which we invite all others, is very simple. It is a fellowship, a family, the faces of Love, committed simply to *living the life of universal, unconditional, forgiving, comforting, healing, supportive, unceasing, visible, sacrificial Love, by sharing it in the family, and by extending it to all of God's creatures and creation.*

So when we invite people to be in the church and to be Christian, we simply invite them to be a part of a loving family, people who are committed to celebrating Love and learning about it, sharing it, and intentionally giving it away. Their membership in a church is not based, then, on completing an official examination on what they know, or on the purity of the theological propositions they affirm or "confess" or believe to be true. They are not even evaluated on the conduct of their lives, how well they display a life of Love. Their only key to full membership in a church should be that they are Loved by God and God's gathered people, along with every other creature, the same as in any other family, and that they want to live a life oriented around Love.

Then, when they are a part of the church, we bring them into the story, the biblical narratives, writings, stories, and songs that give us the words, images, and language to express our deepest encounters with God, and with Jesus, the human face of God, the face of Love, and the narratives that surround him and that define the life God wants for us. Their experience deepens as they come face to face with God, the Source and Creator as well as the presence of forgiving, empowering, supportive, comforting, and challenging Love. We enable them to embrace the elements and traditions of church life, including worship, prayer, meditation, and the historical and theological story of the Christian faith, in an ongoing educational process from a position *inside* the family, fully accepted and fully Loved. This is, in fact, how most people join a church. Most don't join the first day they walk in. They gradually get to know people in the church, spending time getting involved, feeling that they are a part of the people, perhaps joining a group, coming to feel, as many say, "at home." They feel acceptance, they feel a part of things, they come face to face with God; *that is, they come face to face with Love*, God present. Our life together with them deepens our understanding, and theirs, of the importance and centrality of Love in the world, and enables them and all of us to deepen and celebrate the Christian story as our own. But acceptance of the story doesn't come first. Love comes first.

The church is and always has been the vehicle through which the language and stories and images of Love have emerged as the Old and New Testaments. Listening to the Spirit of God, the Spirit of Love, the church wrote the Bible. The church is where words and language in addition to the Bible are formed and reformed, which we often use in our prayers, liturgical formulas, songs, and other elements of church life. The church is the fertile soil where creeds and statements and expressions of Love (sometimes called "theology") are written and rewritten.

The church has fostered and encouraged music and art in praise of God through more forms and styles than you can count. In its structure and polity, it has expanded worshipping communities around the globe for centuries. It has expressed its beliefs and praise in architectural wonders worldwide. The church has built schools and universities and hospitals and orphanages. It has throughout its life ministered to the poor, the homeless, the weak, the lonely, the weary, and the fearful.

The church is where many of life's most significant moments are celebrated. Baptisms, weddings, and memorial services at life's end are all brought into the Loving presence of God in the family of Love. The church helps bring about reconciliations, forgiveness, support, and new beginnings as it extends the Loving presence of the Spirit where the need is great.

Magnificent accomplishments! But the fire behind all of these—their origin, the source of their intention and perseverance—is the Love that is the presence of God. Anything done without it in the name of the church is fatally flawed, and certainly in its long history the church has had its flaws and its moments of shame. But Love is primary in the work of the church. It is the wellspring of all the good the church has done down through the centuries and its inspiration for efforts of loving concern, care, and service that have emerged from its people. It is the birthplace of the joy that is the goal of its proclamation, the joy for which the church yearns and strives for all people and all creation.

Love is first. The Love that is the presence of God is not just another element of the theological hierarchy of the church. Love is its primary essence and power and fuel and joy.

Yet when the church gathers, its conversations tend to revert to topics that are easier to deal with, more concrete, more manageable; for example, what God is *like*, why God does this and not that, how we are to understand God's work, songs and hymns *to* God, and sermons by the score *about* God (I know them; I've preached them). The majority of the creeds and statements and expressions of belief throughout the centuries are centered on the language and images *about* God and Jesus and the Spirit, rather than centering on and expressing the Loving *core* of the faith to which God directs us and wants us to know and live. Much like my dog Frisco, who is more interested in me than in the ball I'm trying to encourage her to find.

It seems to me that we need to talk less about God and more about Love, God's other name!

Now before you set the date for the heresy trial, let me explain more about what I believe that would look like in the life, service, and worship of the church. God *is* Love, so I am convinced that it would enrich our worship, our faith expressions, and people's understanding of the faith by often using God's other name, Love, whenever we can.

For example, I understand how the church's creeds link us to Christians of all ages. I value that link. But instead of reciting, for example, the Apostles' Creed, which is basically a list of things Christians should believe are true *about* God, the faith, and its history and components, it would seem helpful if the church would affirm the core of the faith itself. Maybe like this:

In life and in death, we belong to God,[1] and we trust in
Love.

We affirm that God and Love are one; when we experience Love, we experience God.

We affirm that the Spirit of God speaks through the
Scriptures, revealing the primary truth of the Love
that God wants for all people.

We affirm the presence of the Spirit of God, Love itself
speaking in our world, in all our life experiences
and throughout the universe God has created.

We affirm that Jesus is the human face of Love itself, fully
revealed in his life.

Awakened, filled with the Spirit by the sacrificial death
of Jesus, we affirm that God's gift to the world is
the life of Love itself, eternal and universal. In his
life, ministry, death, and resurrection, Jesus is what
Love looks like, the Love God has created us to live.

Strengthened by the Spirit, we commit ourselves to discovering God's gift of Love itself, orienting our lives
around it, and extending it throughout the world
for the healing, fulfillment, and joy of all life.

We affirm that nothing in this life or in the life of the
resurrection shall ever separate anyone from the
everlasting Love that is God always present with us.

Worship itself is a challenge as well as a joyful celebration for
the church. According to the Pew Research Center, most people
join a new church home because they "*enjoyed the religious services
and style of worship*" there.[2] I realize that the word "enjoy" should
mean something like "it fills me with joy" or "it was such a joyful
experience." I know that. But my experience convinces me that "en-
joyable," in current usage, is often another way to say "entertaining."
Certainly worship experiences need not be negative or tiresome.

1. Presbyterian Church (U.S.A.), *Book of Confessions*, 341.
2. Pew Forum, "Faith in Flux," 19, 29, 33.

But worship services are not entertainment events for people to sit back and either enjoy or reject. The temptation is very real to make worship entertaining and "fun," with cheerful and fun group singing and happy stories, a great band or a perfect choir, avoiding the negative elements such as facing our weaknesses or confessing our misdeeds, or intrusive meditative silence, or anything considered a "downer." Sadly, the idea for many churches seems to be to get more people to *enjoy* themselves when they come, so they'll come again and the church can be a "successful" *institution* with positive membership and strong financial numbers.

Numerous churches have jumped all over this "enjoyment" business and organized their worship and church life accordingly. Some churches, instead of scheduling meetings to plan worship, have "production meetings," as if preparing to put on a good show each week. Of course worship experiences must be carefully planned to be open to the presence of the Spirit, but I believe that although worship for entertainment can really "pack 'em in," it directs attention away from oneself and one's experiences of the Holy along with other worshippers, to the activities "up front," and invites evaluation rather than participation.

Those who come to worship are not there as passive observers to be entertained, as if they were paying customers at a concert. They are active participants seeking a different depth to the experience of Love than entertainment provides. Before they gather for worship, they prepare for it by examining their lives and the world around them, and by bringing their joys and sorrows, hopes and fears, certainties and confusion, and the needs of all humankind into the presence of God, the presence and community of Love itself. They are there to hear *good* news, the proclamation of the simple truth of God's countless free gifts of Love, and to be reminded of (perhaps jerked back into) an awareness of the life of the Spirit as they discover links to those gifts in their own stories. They are there to watch and listen for the voice of God, that is, the presence of Love all around them, to be moved with music and the other arts, and through readings, prayers, sermons, in all the experiences of the Spirit. Sometime in all that, the Spirit's voice will be heard in unexpected ways—a moment of comfort, an insight, a sigh of understanding, a moment of the realization of joy. Worship is spiritual, which means opening oneself to the breath of God, the Spirit, in which the element of entertainment would be intrusive and distracting, and would just be in the way. Worshippers' minds and hearts can be led by careful and creative worship planning to consider and experience the miracle of Love and gratitude to God for the amazing Love God has set loose among them—for the memory of Love in the past, and the joyful hope and expectation of Love in the future for those around them and for themselves— the Love that will not let any of us go.

In worship and beyond, perhaps in groups, a church family can share stories with each other of their encounters with Love, with God, the moments when they have come face to face with the incredible Love of God in their lives, and events and experiences that have touched them deeply. I like the idea of a pastor, after careful planning, saying to the assembled congregation at the beginning of the Sunday service, "Last Sunday at the end of worship I encouraged you to go in peace and serve the Lord. This morning we're going to hear how some of you did that, and how your experience of Love matched your experience of God." I can see members reporting, from then on, periodically, about acts and experiences of Loving care or kindness or some kind of reaching out to another that made a difference in their lives. A cup of coffee enjoyed with an old friend not seen in a long time. An appreciated visit to a nursing home resident. The experience of a volunteer shift at a soup kitchen. A conversation with a stranger in a doctor's waiting room. Taking a grieving friend to lunch or out for a walk. Mowing the yard of a neighbor who is ill. Making a long-term commitment such as joining a group planning to work with city authorities to improve housing opportunities for low-income families, or joining a political campaign, or using influence and contacts to put together a tutoring/support program for youth offenders or kids in danger of dropping out of school. None of these stories or activities would be used to try to manipulate the receiver into coming to church. In fact, in most of the stories I've heard over the years, church and Christianity would usually not be mentioned (although they could be). These acts of the Love would stand on their own and carry their own proclamation of God's presence. All could be specifically identified and celebrated in worship, and would hopefully be the inspiration for others to join in.

These experiences can have a lasting influence, so it is important that leaders are prepared for stories with difficult implications. A group once listened to a young mother of a child who had been in an accident, was in intensive care, and not expected to survive. She reported that she had asked God to make her child well, and the child survived. "God did as I asked," she said. "God is so good." This elicited an angry response from the father of another child who had been ill and for whom he too had prayed, but the child had not survived. The group then took time to talk about prayer, what it was and what it wasn't, to listen to long-held pain and grief, to weep together, to deepen the sense of family for everyone there, and to allow the Love that was God very present and near to go far beyond where the group expected it to be.

God present in Love could become more visible by intentionally reporting, recognizing, publicizing, and talking about simple, everyday events that were moments of Love's presence that happened or were happening in the lives of those who gather. People have stories to tell and want to tell them; all they need is guidance and permission. These stories often turn into larger projects to spread the experience of a Loving God and a Loving church.

In order for Love as God present to be more visible in worship, the biblical stories, songs, and narratives—some of the most beautiful, inspiring, and breathtaking in all literature, and from which sermons and classes are constructed—need to be viewed not as just general moral imperatives or answers to theological questions. They need to be presented as expressions of Loving care, support, and encouragement to all who, at any given moment, are wrestling with an overwhelming sense of the loss of Love in their lives. They need to be clearly presented as to how they enlighten our understanding and experience of Love (which is, in fact, our experience of God), how they suggest loving directions, and how those directions change and enrich the lives of people.

Sermons are sometimes directed to the historical or theological structure of the faith—how a passage of Scripture shows "five attributes of God," or "the meaning of the Trinity" or "how to get to heaven." Sometimes they are organized as what we used to call "straighten up" sermons, such as, "This passage shows that unless you believe certain things are true, or unless you behave yourself, then bad things are going to happen to you" (so "straighten up" and "fly right"!). Once, early in my ministry, I preached a sermon on John Calvin and Martin Luther and the comparison of their views on the birth of the church. I really did. I thought it was wonderful and one of the stellar moments of preaching in the United States. I was sure my seminary church history professor would be impressed. But later, I realized that in that small congregation that morning were: a family grieving over the death of a beloved grandmother killed in an automobile accident in a car driven by her son-in-law, a single mother whose three-year-old child was in the hospital, and an elderly couple whose home they had lived in for forty-eight years had burned to the ground just days before. And those were just the ones I knew about! They didn't need to hear a paper on Calvin and Luther. They needed to hear about, and experience, the Love of a God present in every struggling life, the perfect Love that casts out fear,[3] the Love made visible in my words and experienced in the concrete support of everyone, every practitioner, in that room.

Sermons are not after-dinner speeches or lectures in a classroom. Sermons are the articulation of God's presence, Love itself. Sermons embrace the affirmation that God Loves all people *already*. It is not necessary to form a sermon around what people need to do to convince God to Love them. In fact, I believe that to do so is error, and misses the point of grace. Often the words of the sermon, the good news of God's presence and grace, are extended to people some of whom are existentially unable to believe in the

3. 1 John 4:18.

Love they hear about, so that after the sermon is delivered it is the job of the congregation to bring that sermon—that Love articulated—to life in concrete, Loving, immediate ways to those who need it profoundly and weep for it.

No preacher can get it right every time, and very few are spellbinding orators. But the listener must fight the urge to evaluate or grade a sermon as though it were some kind of entertainment. As the Spirit speaks to us in Scripture, so the Spirit speaks through sermons, even bad ones (yes, there are such things). Consider what is in your mind and heart, what you have brought to worship with you, and listen for what the Spirit of Love might be saying to you as you listen to the Word preached.

Preaching a sermon using a text from the lectionary across its two-year cycle, a text that the preacher has not chosen, is a dangerous, difficult business. But it can be very exciting, because the preacher never knows how the passage will engage him or her. The preacher may approach a passage of Scripture, asking, "Where is the Love in this passage? How is it portrayed in the persons in this passage? What is it like for them; is it hard or is it easy? What is it like for me, the preacher, and what might be the response to it from someone whose life is falling apart and who might not be able to see much Love anywhere, or someone who is overcome by fear, anger, guilt, or loneliness? What form does Love take in this passage, and how might it be portrayed in a situation in a current setting where have I personally seen it or been told about it?" Sermons and other parts of worship, using the same biblical narratives and stories, can explore such themes as "Five new ordinary everyday examples in which the Love God has been experienced specifically in the lives of real people you know," or "Five new specific situations or persons or places that need the attention of your Love, where God is waiting for you," or, even better, "Five new settings or projects that can be established by the church where there is great need, and in which God's Love may be discovered." God is truly as close as the experiences of Love, kindness, forgiveness, justice, and sacrifice—ordinary events as well as spectacular, usually clearly visible, sometimes hidden and later discovered, but all around, every day. To communicate the Christian message in and beyond the church, we need to talk less *about* God, and talk more about what it is like to *know* God, that is, what it is like to *know* Love. Tell stories. Give examples.

It is fairly obvious that throughout history and in the present the Christian church has not always lived out the life of Love. Sometimes it has hid in its buildings, sung its songs, mumbled its creeds and repeated its prayers, and failed to get out and unpack the crates on the dock right there in front of them. In its worship, it has often exchanged inspiration and awe before God for fun and entertainment that will attract more people with the purpose of building a successful institution. It has at times been exclusionary; it has embraced violence, hatred, racism, and bigotry. It has been filled with self-centeredness, hypocrisy, and noisy pride, and talked about its "rights." It has talked about building up its life rather than giving it away. It has anchored its message in fear of hell and manipulation for heaven, and it has set its heart on the institutional accumulation of the wealth and power and the comfort and success of the world (where bigger is always better).

But its center, its core, is and always has been only the life of Love. We church people must free ourselves from our fixations on less important matters, such as which theological systems, beliefs, or ideas are right and which are wrong, which rules the institutional church should follow, how to identify "true" Christians and deal with "sinners," how Christianity should rule society, our political life, and the world, and how to get to heaven. If we can focus instead on living and spreading the central element of Love, irrespective of whether or not the people we touch deserve it, then a hungry world can discover a full and joyful life it never thought possible, and the church would further experience the true euphoria of being "in sync" with all that God wants for us and for all creation. Love is where we will discover joy! When Love happens, joy happens. That's what God wants for all of us.

Over and over down through the years, I have heard it said that people want something they can take home from their church worship and activities. What I think they *should* take home every week is a freshly reported specific *story*. Everybody loves stories; what is television but a box sitting there in your living room to tell you stories? People should leave a worship service with a new awareness of how the persistent, unceasing, unconditional, undeserved, uninterrupted, eternal, universal, forgiving, healing, sacrificial love of God has become visible in their own lives or the lives of people they know in some Loving act. Stories can appear in worship, in a planned group meeting, or in a conversation in the hallway. They are more helpful when they are the kind of daily experiences we all know and have, rather than stories with unusual or dramatic theological overtones. Pictures of Jesus found on a squash from the garden or in a coffee spill on the tablecloth, or a cross-shaped cloud formation, or a voice in thunder are not required. In fact they may turn the storytelling into a competition.

In sharing our common, everyday experiences of Love, all that is needed is something newly discovered (the simpler the better), a new story or an old one, a rediscovered memory or something that happened this morning or yesterday, the discovery of a new hope that will enrich our lives and point us to Love itself. Some I have heard are like this: "I was working so hard planning and organizing my parents' fiftieth anniversary party that by the time the day arrived I was fed up and exhausted, and then I saw them standing there at the reception, and my Love for them was so overwhelming that I could not speak." Or, "I was volunteering at the hospital, and was walking an elderly man from the registration desk to his room, when his eyes clouded up with tears and he took my hand and said in a voice I could hardly hear, "I'm afraid of what may happen to me here," so we stopped at the shop and had a cup of coffee and talked, and I felt like maybe I helped." Or, "My teenage son told me he Loved me. Wow!"

When Love is at the center of the worship and educational life of the church in this way, then it is more easily recognized as the primary motive behind all that happens *outside and beyond* worship services. Wherever they are, Christian people are ministering servants, giving food and blankets to the homebound on a winter's night, or helping the family down the street whose house burned, or the parents of the infant who is mortally ill, or being a friend to runaway teenagers, or helping support work with orphaned children in cities all over the world who roam the streets by the thousands. It has even been suggested, in this period when jobs are scarce, that Christians should use their influence on corporate boards on which they serve to encourage using a portion of profits, and part of the enormous executive compensation and bonuses (surely an executive can make ends meet on five million dollars instead of six for a while), to establish massive training and retraining education efforts for the jobs they have to fill in their own businesses and in others. This need not be just for ultimately higher profits from good workers, but out of a Loving concern for families that need work.

The church's motive in all this is not that we are afraid that God will "get us" if we *don't* do these things, or so that God will be pleased with us and we can then get on God's good side. *Our only motive is that we want Love to be a part of other lives; we want people to know the Love we have been given and that God has already given them and placed within their reach. We want for them all that God wants for all of us: lives enriched, healed, and made new by Love. This is our only goal.* And when we put our trust in Love by engaging in these servant activities, by giving ourselves away, we find a deeper experience of Love, the presence of God waiting for us each time.

We tend to think that this kind of church life is easier in a large church than a small one. I have found that the size of the institution makes no difference whatsoever. Bigger is not better, and it bothers me to hear anyone say that it's so sad that there are so many small churches. In the beginning of this chapter I wrote about my first experience as a pastor of two small congregations. Both churches worked at spreading Love, kindness, and support in their own settings and beyond. I especially remember looking for the first time at the financial records of the smaller of the two. This congregation had just about fifteen faithful members who met to worship together in a small white wooden church building built in 1854 in a quiet pine grove. Their budget was tiny. But beyond their giving to the larger church, world missions, and the like, their books showed expenditures like these: $25 for groceries for Mrs. Parker, $60 to help John Winter rebuild his barn (including men to help), $21.50 for medications for the Sullivan family, $90 for the Williams daughter who was in college, $81 for supplies for the Scott family's new baby (including babysitting), on and on and on, page after page. Almost all of these people who received gifts were not members of that church. They were neighbors in need, and the presence of Love, the voice of God there, was the support of a few dollars, and the personal ministries of the practitioners of God that went along with them.

There are countless stories of Loving care that need to be told in worship and in all the life of the church. Our music, our prayers, our sermons, and our work all need to use God's other name, Love, for not only will it illuminate, bring into focus, and clarify what we are called to do, but as we do it Love will grow among us, and transform us and those God enables us to serve. If we truly want people to *know God*, then we must do all we can so that they come to *know Love (kindness, care, support), for Love is what God is, and although Love and God are identical, "Love," for most people who struggle to understand in these days, is a more easily accessible and visible link to truth and what they are going through than "God"! It is Love that is the primary gift the church has for the world.*

A pastor listened for a long time to a man who was frightened, hurting, and lonely as he told his story of pain and loss. Then the pastor said to him, "The first and most important thing you need to know is that God Loves you. So do I." The man was silent for a moment, head bowed, and then said, "I don't know what you mean when you say God Loves me, but I know what you mean when you say *you* Love me."

The church is where Love, God present, is intentionally made visible. The church, the gathering of the practitioners of Love, is where the ongoing pattern of Love that God the Creator is knitting together for all creation comes into focus. *This is what Christianity is!*

Some time ago, I saw an ad in the paper about a church that listed the minister as the "founding pastor." He was mistaken. The church is not something anyone starts. The church as the gathered body of Love is gathered by God alone. It is not an organization with "founding members." We did not start it, nor can we bring it to an end (which is a great relief to pastors like me, who are sometimes not sure whether our leadership will save the church or destroy it). We join it, we participate in it, we establish expressions of it, and we spread Love through it. It is where two or three are together—or even one—in the act of pouring out Love in the world.

The church is the resurrected living present body of Jesus. It is not an institution, but it is often associated with an organizational element that serves it and supports its work. It is not a building, but it gathers in one from time to time, where its story is presented in art, architecture, symbols, words, songs, prayers, and stories to remind and inspire those gathering there of the power and majesty of the God, the Love, that they serve. "Organization" and "building" and "structure" sound institutional. But we are not trying to build an institution; rather, we are trying to be a part of the revelation and extension of Love, of God, in the world. The church is made up of the faces of Love itself, Love's practitioners. But it is not the only place in this world Love shows its face. Practitioners of Love are everywhere, in and beyond church membership. Love fills creation, waiting to be named and celebrated as life's center and joy. In its life and worship and work the church seeks out, discovers, lifts up, celebrates, and extends as far as it can the countless gifts of Love God has created for every place and person, in every corner of this world.

If you believe that Love, God's other name, is the most important element of human life, and you want to orient your life around it, then you are already one of us.

6

The Book

And the stirring
of the Spirit

IT MAY BE THAT of all the books published throughout history, the Bible may be the most purchased and least read. As a pastor for many years, I have been astounded at the lack of biblical literacy among Christians, from liberals to conservatives, from evangelicals and fundamentalists to mainline Protestants and Catholics, in almost every tradition, including those who claim to believe every word literally as written. And yet, for many who do read it, the Christian Scriptures yield insights, comfort, encouragement, challenges, and new ideas and visions of truth. The Bible is the church's book. It is at the center of the church's life and is the accepted standard for the proclamation of the truth about life by the church to the world. The stories and narratives and writings of the Bible are part of the heart and soul of the Christian experience. According to a 2008 Pew Research Center report, 63 percent of Americans believe the Bible is the "Word of God."[1] But what does it mean that the Bible is authoritative, and is, or contains, as some say, "God's Word"? How is it authoritative? Are the words in this book simply and fully God speaking, God's actual words? How does God, or to put it differently, how does Love speak to us through the Bible?

Certainly there are accounts in the Bible that wouldn't stand up to current scientific standards of expected phenomena or acceptable human relationships. There are certain rules, procedures, and prohibitions in the Bible regarding animal sacrifices, purification of women after childbirth, dietary laws, laws regarding clothing, and many more. There are accounts of God speaking and acting that don't sound very much like a Loving God, such as demands that persons accused of being mediums and wizards be stoned to death,[2] a man being stoned to death for gathering sticks on the Sabbath,[3] or leading people in battle to take over a land where other people lived by means of a deadly war.[4]

Many believe that every word in the Bible should be accepted literally as truth by Christians, as in the bumper sticker, "The Bible says it, I believe it, that settles it!" For this first group, for example, God did make the world in six days,[5] the sun and moon did stop in the heavens when Joshua fought with the Amorites,[6] Jesus did heal people from disease[7] and rose from the dead,[8] and Paul did go to Rome.[9]

Others believe that the Bible should not be understood literally, but that much of it is symbolic story. This second group (these

1. Pew, "U.S. Religious Landscape Survey: Religious Beliefs and Practices," 30.

2. Leviticus 20:6, 27.

3. Numbers 15:32–36.

4. Joshua 1.

5. Genesis 1:1—2:3.

6. Joshua 10:12–14.

7. Mark 3:1–6.

8. John 20:11–18.

9. Acts 28:14.

are representative examples; different people believe different things) understands the first two examples above (creation, the sun and moon stopping) as symbolic stories that didn't really happen that way, but are legends that teach us something about God. There are things they do believe to be true. They find it likely that Jesus taught his followers from a mount, and may have somehow healed people. But they assert that even some of these may be just accounts and descriptive stories that emerged from the early church communities to express and amplify the Love they saw in Jesus' life. They affirm that Jesus somehow appeared to his followers after his death, but the details are hard to uncover, given all the variety of stories people told about those events. The problem for this group, of course, is how to decide what actually happened as written and what didn't, what is symbolic story and metaphor and what is historical fact, and what criteria should be used to determine which is which.

Still others decided that all the scientifically offending passages are not feasible. They may possibly have symbolic value, but none of them happened as written. Thomas Jefferson solved the problem with a pair of scissors (or maybe a knife), excising all the passages that were scientifically acceptable, assembling them together to give him a smoother reading experience.[10] Some people who lean toward this view try to solve the problem by explaining supernatural events in natural terms. For instance, the five thousand people felt so guilty when the boy provided five loaves and two fish that they opened up the food they had brought and there was enough for all.[11] Or, when Jesus healed the man with the demons[12] it was because, many years before, he had studied in Egypt or Rome or somewhere in the Far East, and had learned the secrets of how to heal with certain herbs or compounds. This is simply an attempt to show that these accounts are actually scientifically acceptable after all.

10. Meacham, *Jefferson*, xxi.

11. Mark 6:30–44.

12. Mark 1:21–28.

Whichever way you understand these passages, you are engaging in an important conversation with scientific inquiry, whether that is your intention or not. Either you reject scientific boundaries entirely, and believe what is written is true, and happened as written, or you accept scientific boundaries in interpretation some of the time (some of them happened, but some didn't), or you accept scientific boundaries in every case and reject a significant portion of the biblical material as having no relevance at all, or reinterpret it so that it fits in a scientific worldview.

The crucial implication of entering into this conversation with science (which, remember, we enter whether we want to or not) is that we must accept one of the universal guidelines of scientific inquiry, which is that the possibility always exists that there will be discoveries, evidence, developments, or ideas somewhere in the future that may or will invalidate previous conclusions. It happens all the time; it has already happened. For example, the assumption of the biblical writings is that the universe is constructed of three stories or levels, with the heavens above, the earth in the middle, and Sheol, the place of the dead, below. Subsequent scientific discoveries and studies have invalidated that view and new discoveries about the universe are constantly evolving. Biblical writers wrote accounts and stories of their experience of the Holy using the scientific contexts and language that they knew. Did they mean for us to accept their science as part of their encounter with the truth about God? Is God only available to us through first-century science? Who knows what evidence is yet to be discovered in our world that will impact and mold our understanding of what is written in the Bible? Who knows how many earthen jars filled with written treasure are still hidden in the deserts of the Middle East?

To persons "unaffiliated" with religion, this whole struggle Christianity has with scientifically questionable events in the Bible presents major roadblocks. They can't comprehend why they should have to suspend their scientific and technological worldview in order to be Christian, and in certain passages affirm a first-century science and worldview that has no place in the rest of their experience.

We need to look at the Bible differently. In reading it, the point is not so much a question of objective data, of making an objective intelligent choice about what is true and what is not true, what happened and what didn't, or even how it happened. Rather I am convinced that the function of the Bible, in the inspiring beauty and depth of its people, narratives, and stories, is to serve as a vehicle through which the Spirit of God, the Spirit of Love, speaks to the church and its people and to all who read it carefully. This is what it means that the Bible is "inspired," that the Spirit, "the breath of God," is *constantly* breathing through it and into the hearts of those who read it. The Spirit is not confined to the words of the Bible or limited by it, its worldview, its science, the ethics of its personalities, or its cultural structures. The Bible wasn't just inspired once, and isn't being inspired anymore. God's Holy Spirit, Love breathing, comes to us continually through Scripture and defines, enlightens, and enlivens our connection to Scripture and our understanding of it.

God is Love, and Love (God present with us) always precedes and enlightens our understanding of Scripture, and calls for and clarifies our Loving response.

The Spirit may come to the church and its people as an insight, an idea, or a truth about life in the world. It may come as a challenging life correction, a comfort, or an answer to a question or a prayer. It may appear as an encouragement, or as a gift of peace. In fact the Spirit's voice speaking through the Bible is all these things to millions of people, and has always been so.

The church has understood this primary emphasis on the Spirit, in the life of the church, from the beginning. In fact, there was a time during the earliest life of the church, from its initial days and months down through its first decades, when there was no Bible at all for the Christian church. The Torah, the Prophets, and the Writings of Israel were there for those who had been Jews, but the New Testament was far in the future. In the weeks and months following the cross and resurrection, there was no authoritative, objective data or instructions written down to clearly define the new church. There were only strong leaders, and as time and decades went by, a few letters, papers, stories, and personal accounts sent from congregation to congregation to encourage and to teach. Not all of the new churches would have received all the letters that were available. Since the Christian communities began to be spread out from Rome to Egypt and even beyond, it is realistic to assume that a variety of different emphases and stories and ways to talk about the Christian faith grew up in different locations.

But from the beginning, the new church had all it needed, the most important guide of all. The church lived in the power of the Spirit, rather than a recognized, authoritative, and approved Scripture. The Spirit was a power that was continually undergirding the new church, wherever it may have been. It was not until several hundred years into its history, when councils of the church began to gather these papers, narratives, and stories together, that the church began to embrace a Bible. Even then, its authority was slow to evolve, and although it began to be gathered into a collection early, the collection of the books of the Bible (the canon) was not officially defined by the Roman Catholic Church until the Council of Trent in 1545. By that time, the Reformation churches began to define the extent and limits of the Bible for themselves, as the early church fathers had gradually begun to do centuries before.

All through its history, the Spirit has always preceded Scripture, and the church has depended on the Spirit to understand Scripture. Especially throughout the Reformation and since, the new Protestant church affirmed that the Bible, as the Word of God or the revelation of God or the witness of God, depends on the presence of the Spirit to be authoritative. The 1646 Westminster Confession (ch. 1) states that "our full persuasion and assurance of the infallible truth and divine authority thereof [i.e., Holy Scripture as the Word of God], is from the inward work of the Holy Spirit, bearing witness by and with the Word in our hearts."[13]

In The Confession of 1967 (9.30), the Presbyterian church declared, "God's word is spoken to his church today where the

13. Presbyterian Church (U.S.A.), *Book of Confessions*, 122–23.

Scriptures are faithfully preached and attentively read in dependence on the illumination of the Holy Spirit . . ."[14]

In the 1991 Declaration of Faith (10.4), the Presbyterian Church reaffirmed that, "The same Spirit who inspired the prophets and apostles rules our faith and life in Christ through Scripture . . ."[15]

The United Methodist Doctrinal Standards, in the Confession of Faith of The Evangelical United Brethren Church (IV), affirms that the Bible "is to be received through the Holy Spirit as the true rule and guide of faith and practice,"[16] and that we open our hearts and our minds to receive it.

The North American Lutheran Church Confession of Faith states this about the Scriptures of the Old and New Testament: "Inspired by the Holy Spirit speaking through their authors, they record and announce God's revelation centering in Jesus Christ. Through them the Holy Spirit speaks to us to create and sustain Christian faith and fellowship for service in the world."[17]

All these indicate that we find the truth of God in Scripture *as the Spirit opens it up to us.* The Bible is not just an intellectually challenging puzzle or objective answer book, complete in itself, so that by unlocking its secrets through our intellectual efforts we can find a passage that will magically answer our homework questions, or tell us which apartment to rent, or which solution to choose at work. Rather, it is a living, holy document that derives its Holiness as God's Spirit speaks through it a Word of truth and Love to the reader.

Therefore, we are not so much looking for what the Bible itself says; we are listening for what God says through the Bible. We make that discovery of the Spirit not just studying Scripture with our minds but also by listening for the Spirit with our hearts in the words of the Bible.

---

14. Ibid, 257.

15. Ibid, 268.

16. United Methodist Church, *Book of Discipline*, 71.

17. North American Lutheran Church, "Confession of Faith," #3.

Sometimes, personal feelings and experiences we bring to the interpreter's table have a way of overshadowing the sound of the Spirit in Scripture. The danger is that we will assign to Scripture ideas and beliefs that we already embrace, and for which we seek validation. From the European settling of the new world in the seventeenth century, scores of American Christian churches saw in Scripture the justification for slavery and White supremacy. That, they said, is what the Bible teaches.[18] That interpretation rose from accepted social settings, which found support in some literal biblical writings. This use of the Bible to back up our opinions is still around, as various political and social issues are assigned religious support from the Bible in order to establish a kind of social "respectability." This is supposed to bring about desired results in public opinion and policy, such as in the discussions of homosexuality, capital punishment, and the role of women. Often what we hear the Spirit saying in Scripture is challenging our own feelings, pushing us beyond them, listening for the God of Love, who makes all things new. It helps to remember that a hundred years from now (maybe sooner than that) our descendants will be looking at some of our interpretations of Scripture, just as we ourselves are looking back, asking themselves, "What could they have been thinking to have interpreted the Bible to be saying that?" After all these centuries, did we really think that our conclusions would be the final theological word?

How then do we know that the "Word" we hear coming to us *through* the Bible as we read it is actually the Spirit of God, and not just what we want to hear or already believe? How do we go about listening for the Spirit in Scripture?

First, read and study Scripture with others as well as alone. For years, I have been a part of a study group that meets for an hour for breakfast every Thursday morning, to be together, to pray together, and to study the passages to be used in worship the following Sunday. I like to spend time alone studying Scripture, and I consider that time of quiet reading and thinking infinitely valuable. But I consider what has emerged in our morning conversations to

18 Smith, et al., *American Christianity*, 2:177.

be enlightening, inspiring, and corrective for my private study, and often opens doors for me that needed opening, and gives me a needed push through them. Christian truth is not a private affair. Biblical interpretation is done by the church as a whole, not just by individuals, in order to correct or change or enhance our understanding, and to take our human imperfections into account. We must always be ready to have even our most cherished ideas and conclusions questioned and rejected, not just affirmed, as the Spirit makes its way through the words of Scripture.

Second, we have to approach the Bible prepared. Before you open Scripture, carefully and honestly consider what is happening in your own life. What are the joys and the despair, the happiness and the pain, the dark times, the fears and the sorrows that are deep inside you? What is going on in your life? What are the one or two or three really painful or baffling problems you face? What are your moments of sadness, the ways in which you hurt? What are the hard decisions before you? What are the experiences of guilt or anguish or confusion? What are your deep concerns beyond you own understanding? It has been my experience that it helps to bring these to Scripture (and definitely to worship, too) intentionally, rather than coming empty, expecting to be filled automatically (although sometimes it happens that way too). When the hard things are there, awake in my consciousness, and I'm aware of them, then I hear the Spirit in the words and images and messages of the Bible, as though God had connected me to the language of Love I need to hear.

Third, we listen for the Spirit speaking in the Bible by careful, honest study of the whole Bible. The church has always believed that listening for the Spirit means using our minds, digging into the passage carefully, using original languages, understanding the full historical and biblical context. Listening to the Spirit means discovering what the societal norms were like when it was written, how the images and ideas were understood by the original listeners, and what the words meant when they were first written in classical as well as colloquial use.

Fourth, understand that discovering the Spirit speaking through the Bible is never as simple as letting the Bible fall open somewhere, and blindly putting our finger down on a passage and expecting to hear God's voice. Use of a lectionary, a collection of passages from throughout the Bible set in a two-year reading schedule, is essential, so that readers don't stay with those passages that are most familiar. The passage must be read over and over, *each time more slowly than the last*, one word at a time, one phrase at a time, as new, exciting, and stimulating ideas begin to unfold, with challenging new possibilities for the meaning of the passage (this has been particularly helpful to me). Do not be lulled by easy pat solutions. Don't skim quickly over passages you think you already know. Remember, the Spirit is speaking through the Bible, and God always has something new to say. I must confess, I Love to do this kind of work!

Fifth, remember that the most important way to listen for the voice of the Spirit in the Bible is to never forget that the "Word" that God "speaks" in the Bible is Love. In fact it is not just a word that God speaks; it is who God *is*. Scripture is the church's standard of what Love is, and Love is the one consistent truth that runs unfettered throughout the Bible. We can readily understand and identify with the Love contained in its narratives and its images, as we connect *our* stories with the stories there. Even when events are recorded as moments of God's anger, it is anger at the apparent failure of Love to fully alter the direction and character of human freedom, which is itself bound to imperfection and brokenness. Christians call this situation human "sinfulness," the apparent absence and the loss of Love; it simply means we are imperfect and we know it. The supposed anger of God is, in fact, a component of God's benevolent Love. We know what it is to Love and be angry at the same time. It is God's *Love*, not God's supposed anger and wrath, that never ends (see 1 Corinthians 13:8).

So we look for the role of Love in every part of Scripture—persistent, unconditional, undeserved, unselfish, forgiving, healing, sacrificial, universal Love. We ask of every passage we read:

> *How does this passage illuminate and reveal the Love that*
> *is God, the Love that is already present in the world, the*
> *love that God wants for me and all humankind?*

Sixth, interpretive work is never finished until we discover the Spirit of God infusing the passage with power for us *beyond* the printed words. This is a step beyond the excitement we feel when we successfully "unpack" a passage, and discover the true meaning and implications of the words, the literary context, and all the rest. We finally hear the voice of the Spirit for our time, when we understand the deeper tones of Love in the passage, touching the church and each of us in our hearts as well as our minds, meeting us in our own lives and circumstances. This is how we discover the Spiritual authority, the Spirit of Love speaking *through* Scripture.

To be honest about all this, we must recognize that some passages in Scripture do not seem to reflect the loving grace of God or the Word of Love that God speaks. Listening for and hearing the voice of the Spirit flowing through particular passages of Scripture, passages that seem to do violence to the Loving purposes of God for all creation, are the most difficult to understand. When a passage does not appear to express or reflect the multifaceted Love of God for all people and all creation, I confess that it is difficult for me to hear the Spirit speaking through it. When I read that when an army of Israel captures a town the commandment is to kill all the young men in that town,[19] or that when parents believe that their son is stubborn and rebellious, a glutton and a drunkard, they are commanded to deliver him to the elders, who are to stone him to death,[20] then it is hard for me to hear the Spirit of God's Love emerging through that passage. When I read about those who have resisted the Loving truth, whose lives have turned toward violence

19. Deuteronomy 20:13.

20. Deuteronomy 21:20.

or hatred or selfishness or the savage inflicting of pain on another, who have been lost and destroyed in pain forever, it is hard for me to hear the Spirit of God's redeeming, recreating, unending Love there. When I think of those who know Love and its power, but by different names and stories and categories than ours, who are to be consigned to eternal punishment,[21] I find it hard to hear the voice of the Loving Spirit there.

But we cannot automatically reject these passages outright. Rather, we continue to listen for the Spirit's presence throughout Scripture, which the church has affirmed as its primary witness to God's Loving presence in all the experiences of life (including the difficult ones). We come back to them again and again. Such passages either reveal the Love of God in unexpected ways, perhaps understood in historical or social settings that I find hard to comprehend, or they become incomprehensible and unintelligible for me for a time, and exist in mystery. We cannot ignore them; for God's Spirit is free, and the Spirit will speak through them in ways we cannot fully fathom. Rather, for a time, right now, in the present, we simply don't understand them. We wait for God's Spirit to open them up to us, when the time is right, when we will at last understand their role in the full Loving providence of God.

The Bible was written over a long period of years by many different writers in many different cultural settings, and its authority does not rest in itself and in our ability to understand it fully and correctly. The contrasting Gospel accounts of the resurrection alone should convince us that all its parts are not themselves in total agreement or accord. Certainly, it is important to study the Bible carefully with all the interpretive tools available to us. The more we do that work of serious Bible study, and the more we bring ourselves honestly before Scripture, then the more we hear the voice of Love in what we read there.

But it is the Spirit speaking to us *through* the Bible that is authoritative, not the Bible by itself. We need to be able to hear what the *Spirit* is saying to us in Scripture, rather than finding a sentence somewhere in the text that seems to answer our questions,

21. Matthew 25:46.

or worse, give us permission to engage in activities that may be unLoving and unGodly. God's Spirit, God's Breath, God who is Love, is the life and power of the Bible. Therefore we must take care that the book itself, as an instrument of witness and revelation, does not become more important in our lives than that to which it witnesses, and the simple truth it reveals.

We do not worship the Bible; we worship only God. We are not looking for what the Bible says, but rather what God says through the Bible. God speaks to us through the Bible as the Spirit (Love) breaks through and out of the Bible's words, sometimes leaving them behind, touching us in the deepest unknown corners of our hearts.

I am convinced that we are given a kind of "receiver mechanism" inside us to hear the Spirit's voice. God has put it there. According to Jeremiah, God has written a new covenant on our *hearts* so that we may respond to God. [22] It is God who has given us a new *heart*,[23] just so that we may recognize the Spirit's voice. The ability to recognize the breath of the Spirit is not in ourselves that we can brag about our powers of seeing and listening and hearing. We recognize this voice of God only because we have been awakened and reawakened to life by the Spirit.

We need to take our weakness and our imperfection into account when attempting to listen to the Bible this way. There will be times when men and women of good will hold different, sometimes opposite affirmations of the voice of the Spirit on particular questions and issues. *There may be some questions we can't resolve! Yikes!* When this happens, the solution is mutual respect and ongoing persistent searching and listening. Even when all are in agreement, it is not the time for self-congratulation for having "broken the code" of the Spirit's voice in Scripture. Rather, what are called for are humility and thanksgiving and ongoing persistent searching and listening. We cannot ever assume we have cornered all truth. We can, however, celebrate Love discovered, live it, spread it around, and keep listening.

22. Jeremiah 31:33.
23. Ezekiel 36:26.

The voice of the Spirit is not limited to the Bible. We do not have the Spirit cornered there. The Bible remains the standard focus for listening to the Spirit, but God's Spirit speaks constantly all around us. The Spirit is at work in *all* of life's experiences, which is how they become meaningful, instructive, and authoritative. The more we are able to recognize the work of the Spirit in the world around us, the more we can discover it present in Scripture. The more we hear it in Scripture, the more we find it all around us. Whenever authentic, persistent, unceasing, unconditional, undeserved, eternal, universal, forgiving, healing, sacrificial Love is visible in our experience, there is the Spirit of God.

The Spirit is here at the miracle of childbirth, when God breathes the first holy breath into those tiny lungs. The Spirit is here hiking through the glorious West Virginia spring-green forests. The Spirit is here when two old friends set up a checkerboard in the park on a warm summer afternoon, and when a young Palestinian woman becomes the first in her family to graduate from college. The Spirit is here on a silent, snow-covered, moonlit night, when a homeless family finds shelter and a hot meal in a church basement. The Spirit is here in the giggle of a three-year-old recovering from tuberculosis in a hospital in Sudan, and in the embrace of a father for his son come home from war. The Spirit is here on a midnight Appalachian mountaintop, gazing up at a billion billion stars (by actual count!), and when a loving arm encircles grieving trembling shoulders. The Spirit is here when fresh clean water from a system of wells and irrigation begins to flow in a rural African village, and when the documents of international peace and justice are finally signed by all the nations (dream on, Father Martin!).

The Spirit flows where it will. Moving through the Bible, the Spirit opens our hearts to the Love in the world all around us, and to Love's power there. We discover in our own experience the presence of a loving God, a power of Love far beyond our making or our understanding, which is enriched by our study of Scripture. This is how we know that God is real—not by proofs, not by trying to convince ourselves intellectually, not by understanding scientifically, not by self generated or even spontaneous emotional experiences, but by meeting God in all those experiences of Love, where God's/Love's Spirit is at work in Scripture, in the church, and in all of life. When you know Love, you know God. This is how we know God, through the flow of the Spirit, the flow of Love, in life's deepest moments. God is a God of history, in biblical history, in our history, working in and around us for Loving purposes— sometimes gloriously bright, sometimes distorted as if in a reflection in a carnival funhouse mirror. Sometimes we can only catch partial glimpses of God's purposes.

But we do affirm this: *what we are seeing, even in those times when it is not clear, is that the particular kind of persistent, unconditional, undeserved, unselfish, forgiving, healing, sacrificial, universal Love we discover in the stories, the accounts, and ideas of the Bible, and the breathtaking Love we experience in this world around us, are in fact together the holy presence and loving grace of God for all people, and all creation.* This Love is there for them and for all of us, whether we recognize it or not. It is God's Spirit breathing the life of Love into us and into the entire world. This is in fact what God wants for us and has always wanted for us and our sisters and brothers in every land. This is what God is pointing to and has always been pointing to. This Christian proclamation of Love touches our hearts, engages our minds, and makes perfect sense. The living and the sharing of this Love are the substance of Christianity in its simplest form. This Love is what the stories and teachings of the Bible are about. The presence of Love is the lens through which the Bible comes alive for us—a Love to celebrate, to share, to give away, to spread to the farthest boundaries of life. The orientation of our lives around this Love is the presence of joy.

7

The Story

And the Love that
truly wins

Grace

CHRISTIANITY PRESENTS ITSELF THROUGH its story, its family history. It is the narrative expression of how the church talks about the way the Spirit of Love has worked its way through our lives from the beginning. It's simply the story of God's Love in all its forms. It's the story in our long human saga of how God's Loving presence upholds, transforms, and enriches all our journeys to bring us home.

The essence of the story is much the same as the story of your history with your young child (if you don't have a child, use your imagination). *Now hang in there with me here, because this is important.* It begins with how your young child learns who you are. This may happen by your sitting your child down and telling him or her who you are, where you came from, what you do for a living, what your favorite food is, and what are the rules he must learn to live by. I'm aware there are many for whom this is mistakenly perceived of as a good shortcut to parenthood; you may want to write it all down for him, then he will get it all straight and know all *about* you. But that's not the way it usually happens. Love precedes all this. Love comes first. At some point, early on, he will recognize your great power over him, that you are bigger than he is, that he lives in your world, and that you are in charge. He may want to know what he must do to please you, what you are like, and how much he can get away with. He may want to know who you want him to be and what you want him to do. The temptation here is to simply spell it out for him.

But when you show your Love for him not based on anything he has done well or not done, when you create an Eden-like experience for him, when you get down on the floor and play with him, and smile at him, and listen to him, and hug him and calm his fears, and make the hurt go away, he discovers how satisfying and pleasing and good this relationship is. Simultaneously, he learns that this is what you want *for* him, that this is who you really are, and that the boundaries (which are invariably broken) and what pleases you (which he may not always accomplish) and what you want him to be and do (which he may never really be or do) are not as important, not as basic and enduring, as the discovery that he has made. He has discovered that he can look ahead to a warm, Loving, caring, safe, consistent, forgiving relationship with you, and he can live each day without fear, fully trusting you in the certainty of your unending Love for him. He can come at last to understand that nothing he will ever do will make you stop Loving him. Then perhaps he will even *want* to please you in his Love responding to *your* Love, which always comes first. You are the one who Loves him first (even in those times when he doesn't seem to Love you very much), the one who wants for him that great Love filling his life. You are the one who is always there for him, who listens to him, who laughs and cries with him, the one who wants for him that strong sense of being Loved and supported. You are dependable. You are the one he comes to when there is trouble, you are the one who sets safe boundaries and helps him understand consequences, you are the one who wants for him a deep sense of security and safety. As this relationship grows, it becomes clear to him that the things you want for him are things like happiness, generosity, humility, a sense of self-worth, joy, friend-ship, concern for others, unselfishness, discipline, creativity, a deep sense of justice and fairness, security, courage, peace, Love—all the things he has seen in you.

In the first instance, if you just try to sit him down and tell him about yourself, the child will learn *about you*, but secondly, she or he will learn *who you truly are*. What we learn *about* God, just as what we learn *about* our parents, is more quickly forgotten in the long run, and perceived of as less important than the relationship of Love that grows between parents and children, and between all of us and God. I do not know what the farm looked like where my father grew up in upstate New York, and there are a lot of details about his and my mother's lives I do not know or remember. Sometimes their skills as parents were not perfect. But I know that their Love for my brothers and me was true and strong. I know it from our life together and from what they wanted for us, and what they were willing to do to make it happen. "Knowing *about*" is not knowing.

The reason for all this about you and children is that *here is the essence of the Christian story*—how God came down to the floor and played with us, smiled and Loved us, and how we discovered the presence of dependable, trustworthy Love among us, all the Love God wanted and wants *for* us. The experience of this kind of Love within the human community is the way we come to discover God. It is where we hear the "voice" of God, whether it is the Love of a mother for an infant, a child for a grandparent, a friend for a reconciling friend, a child for a puppy, a groom and a bride for each other, a father for a wounded weeping child, a student for an inspiring class, a musician for a symphony, or an early riser for dawn on a mountain summit. Discovering Love is how we come to know that God "is." In our experience of Love, we are drawn to its Loving source, God the creator of all that is and the creator and giver of this Love, the "the Love behind our Loves / the life infusing all our lives."[1] This is how we define "God." This is how God is Love.

The language and stories of the Christian faith found in the Bible, faithfully written and produced by the church over many centuries, are the language and stories of Love in all its forms—the same Love experienced by all people everywhere, not just by Christians, not just by religious people. It is the creative, faithful Love in Scripture that expresses for us what we have seen and experienced in our lives. In the narratives of the Christian faith Love is given a name and a story around which Christians gather. In the stories of the Christian faith a beginning and a future of Love are named. An origin and a creator of Love are recognized and affirmed. Accounts of Love's success and failure fill the history of our faith. But it is our experience of this Love that leads us to affirm and revere its creator and source.

The Christian story is the call of God to trust Love and live fully in God's perfect Love. In telling and retelling the Old Testament narratives, the life of Jesus, the events of the cross and resurrection, and the life of the new church, and in all the events of Love in which *we* engage, we discover over and over that this Love that gives us life is a *gift* from God, from Love itself. It is a gift we had no part in creating and one that we in no way deserve. God Loves all creation's children and all creation itself, simply because it was a Loving God who brought them into being. This benevolent God is *for* you, not out to get you, not withholding Love for a later decision about you. This Love is not dependent on your resume or your income, your family ties or your connections, your success or your failure, your fears or your struggles, the quality of your life, or your past or your dreams. Love will have its way, and it is already yours. It will never end. It will never let you go.

"But surely," you say, "I must do *something* to be a part of this story and receive God's Love! If good works don't earn me the Kingdom, then it must be that all I have to do is come to Jesus, or call on Jesus, or affirm that Jesus is the son of God, or ask for

---

1. Bowie, "Memorandum on Mortality," 21.

forgiveness, or 'do my part' [whatever that may be], or 'reach out an accept it.' Surely there is *something* I must do, *something* I *can* do." But every time you find something you feel you must do to be a recipient of the sacrificial love of God, you are trying to take control again, you are desperately trying to deserve it, and you are trying to be the one in charge of your own salvation, your own destiny. You want to own it; you want to be responsible for it yourself. You want to be a self-made man or woman. It is hard to let go, to allow God to be the one in charge, to trust the power of Love as the way life is to be lived and where life is found, and to simply allow the gift to come to you and fill you. Sometimes we do come to Jesus, sometimes we do ask for forgiveness, sometimes we do call on God for help. But these are not to change God's mind about us somehow, to get God to Love us when before God did *not* Love us. God already Loves us, all of us, all of creation. God *is* Love! Love has always been there for us, and for all people, in all its faces, and always will be there, not because of us or anything we do or don't do, but because of God.

This is what Christians call *grace*, one of the primary categories of the Christian story, the Love from God that is absolutely free. Whenever you hear someone say to you, "All you have to do is . . ." about receiving the Loving grace of God, then you know that grace which is truly free has been tragically abandoned.

For most of us, receiving any gift is a real problem, one of the most difficult of all human experiences. We have to justify getting a gift by trying to figure out a good reason why we deserved it in the first place, or by returning a gift in kind to the giver, so that the balance is restored, and neither of us is in the debt of the other, and we are still sadly separated from each other. If I invite you to dinner, you feel you have to return the favor. If I get a Christmas card from you, I immediately try to get one back to you before Christmas, if there is time. If you give me a birthday present, I can't rest until I'm sure I have you on my calendar, to get you one from me.

But grace, Love, means receiving a gift from God that we do not deserve, that we cannot purchase, that we cannot equal in some kind of return gift. "Who has given a gift to God," writes Paul rhetorically in his letter to the Roman church "to receive a gift in return?"[2] No one! God cannot be bought. The gift has been freely given, like the ideal Love from a parent to a child, and Love will have its way.

Beginnings

Love is there from the Bible's first chapter, in the nature of the creation itself, when the man and the woman find themselves in a beautiful abundant garden only as a result of God's Love for them and for the world (not because they have done anything to deserve it).[3] We tend to forget about Eden as a source for the Spirit speaking to us, since Adam and Eve were sent out of it, but the garden God made is still there. The four rivers that flow out of Eden are even now still flowing, enriching us with the Loving essence of the garden, and reminding us of the garden world God made and how God still wants the world to be. This garden is how the new life will be in the end when all things will be made right, and universal perfect Love is established. When we try to grasp the long-ago real existence of such a place with our *minds*, we struggle, and endure great controversy among religious people. But our *hearts* recognize Eden immediately. Just as it was a part of the early history of the human family, so many of us, too, remember the Eden-like safety and Love of infancy and childhood. We remember not with our minds, but with our hearts, and although often factually inaccurate (things were not always idyllic in our versions of *Little House on the Prairie*), still often there are true memories and stories of warm, safe, Loving beginnings, or Loving moments that make their way into life later, as new beginnings. Eden was like that for the human family. Recognizing Eden both at the beginning of our lives and since enables us to identify with the Bible, and see our own stories there, and extend that healing Love to those who have

2. Romans 11:33–36.

3. Genesis 1–3.

not experienced Eden, or have not been able to see it anywhere in their lives.

The Love of God continues throughout the Bible's story. When God chose Abram, it was not that Abram was being rewarded for being good, or even faithful. In fact, he was involved in some questionable events later in his life. But God was faithful to him as promised. Abram's assigned task was to bring the people of the earth back to God, back to the blessing, back to an Eden-like life of Love and peace.[4] Over and over, this God of Love reached out to a lost and disobedient people, to bring them back home, to covenant with them, to establish lives of fairness, truth, justice, fullness, and peace. God never chose the Hebrew people simply to lift them up as privileged and apart from the other nations. They were chosen to be used to bring the rest of humanity back to that life of Love, back to God. That meant *all* the nations, *all* the people of the earth, for God created and Loved them *all*. Through the history of the Hebrews, including slavery and later exile, the Love that was God was always with them. God was always faithful. The Love of God for all people and all creation is the continuing thread that runs through the Bible, the one truth that our minds can see and analyze, and our hearts can grasp and feel and celebrate.

Life Revealed

Christians have always understood that the central focus of the story, from beginning to end, is Jesus, in whom God's Loving Word of creation first spoken in Genesis became visible once again. He is God's Word, Love's face. This is why so many people were and are drawn to him. He is what God has to say, a new creation given a human face.

In his life, ministry, death, and resurrection, the truth of God's *Love* was fully pictured, fully present, set in the center of all humanity to show again, finally, how much and how deeply we are Loved by God, in spite of ourselves, our weaknesses, and our

4. Genesis 12:1–3.

imperfections. The one great central creative power of the universe is truly benevolent. Those of us who have been deeply Loved by another, or have deeply Loved another, can only imagine, in comparison, how much *more* we are Loved by God, and how much *more* God as perfect Love itself surrounds us, and draws us into its power with all human kind and all creation. *Our* experience of Love helps us understand, at least in part, the enormity of *God's* Love—perfect Love itself—for all of us.

The events in the life story of Jesus trigger this recognition. He spoke of and lived Love. The stories the church preserved show him healing the sick, raising the dead, walking on water over the deep, where demons lived, to go to frightened disciples in a boat, feeding hungry people from a few loaves and some fish, all to show what the Love he embodied looked like, not just for the Jews but for all the world's people, and to bring them back home.[5] His job was to be a *revelation*, a picture, of the Love that God has placed in creation, which is the most important thing in the world. *How* he did it is not the point. The whole point was to present a picture of himself as the embodiment of the same active providential Love that God had for the world all throughout Israel's history.

As I indicated above, the question of how he did it triggers the interest of the *scientific mind*, but whenever you try to determine whether something happened or not, or how it happened, you are asking for a solution that requires an explanation by scientific evidence. And whenever you decide something by evidence, you must recognize that there may be evidence out there somewhere that may show up one day to prove the opposite. But in reading the church's story in the Bible, the authority for its truth is not in knowing, "Yes, it happened that way" or "No, it didn't happen that way." The authority for truth in the Christian story is the Spirit speaking in and through it to our hearts. The truth is what is behind these stories, and from which they spring. It is the Loving-kindness that surrounded Jesus' healings, the expression of Love in his teachings, the Loving care and forgiveness and encouragement revealed in his journey through Palestine, and finally his Loving sacrifice

5. These accounts are found throughout Matthew, Mark, Luke, and John.

that trigger the *heart*, now just as then. They weren't "neat tricks." They were teachings. His life, what he did, taught something, and revealed something. He was telling them, "Love has always been here, and Love heals. You don't have to be afraid or alone anymore. You are, and have always been, in the presence of a Loving God who will never let you go."

No Greater Love

The supreme moment in Jesus' life was his death. The definitive statement of the meaning of the cross is found in the Gospel of John, in the words of Jesus:

> "*No one has greater Love than this,*" he said, "*to lay down one's life for one's friends.*"[6]

The greatest expression of Love, that is, the moment of God's clearest and greatest presence, was when a person gave up his or her life for another. The immediate story presents his arrest, trial, and crucifixion. Even though they all abandoned him, and Peter denied even knowing him, and they all went fearfully into hiding, he did not give them up to the authorities. In the Gospel of John, he is even recorded as saying to the Roman soldiers arresting him, "I am the one you want; let these men go."[7] He had been showing them the life of Love for three years, and now he was to show them the greatest possible Love. Now he had his moment. Now was his time. He sacrificed his life for them, saved them from the fury of the mob, and, through the legal system, he also gave up his life for Barabbas,[8] *to visibly show the love beyond which there is no greater Love.* But there is a deeper story beyond the immediate participants. There are a variety of "theories" of the effect of the cross and the crucifixion on us living centuries later who were not there. Some think it provided a "good moral influence" on all people throughout history, that they would see what Jesus did,

6. John 15:13.
7. John 18:8.
8. John 18:39–40.

and say, "I too should be prepared to die for someone if it ever becomes necessary," or at least "I too should be good, unselfish, dedicated and Loving in my own life." Others believe that Love was actually created at that moment, that it moved life from law in the Old Testament to Love in the New. Still others believe that it was necessary for God to be satisfied and appeased (mirroring the sacrificial rites of the Jews of that time, setting things right with God by offering a sacrifice seeking forgiveness to show they really meant it). Someone had to be punished for all the sin and sins in the world; God couldn't let humankind get away with sin. Jesus took the punishment that it was necessary for God to dole out. This is the perspective that is summarized, "Jesus *had* to die for you." We may wonder who thought up those unLoving, chilling rules that God was "forced" to follow. If forgiveness was to come out of this, why not just forgive, without violence to Jesus or anyone? Or, since forgiveness and salvation were to be the result, does it mean then that we believe that human sacrifice to receive God's Love is indeed effective to that end? It seems to have worked pretty well that time. There are other theories that are variations of these, including the theory that Jesus' death was a payment from God to Satan to buy back humankind from sin, in which God tricked Satan into thinking Jesus was permanently dead, and instead he was raised on the third day.

It should be a great embarrassment to the church that these remain theories, and that there was and is no universal agreement about the meaning of the central moment in the Christian faith. I believe the many possibilities of what this "atonement" means is a result of an attempt to explain Christianity logically, legally, scientifically, in the thinking mind; to solve a puzzle, rather than to look to the Spirit, to what the heart perceives in the cross. Although the Spirit touches us in our minds as well as our hearts, our hearts are its primary target. The Spirit touches us at this sacrificial death just as when we are touched when anyone else gives up his or her life for another, and uncovers the truth that life's meaning is found in the life of Love, the greatest of which is sacrificial Love.

The sacrificial death of Jesus was a *revelation*, the revelation of God, which is the revelation of Love, and all that God wants for us. A revelation is an *uncovering*. It is the uncovering of something that was hidden, but something that was always there. The uncovering doesn't create the thing that was previously covered. It is inaccurate to conclude that when Jesus died God finally started Loving us and caring for us and finalized our destinies, and that to receive that Love and that destiny, you have to do or say or believe certain things. It isn't that God's Love for us was *created* at that moment. It was always there. The sacrificial death of Jesus simply and yet majestically enabled Love to be visible and effective in our lives, the same way a painting exists under a cover. It doesn't come into being when it is uncovered for the first time, but it does begin to touch people; it becomes effective. A new piece of music exists on a piece of manuscript before it is played or performed, but when it is played it is uncovered, it comes alive, and it touches the lives around it, and changes people. It becomes effective. The life and ministry and teachings and miracles and healings and Love of Jesus are an *uncovering*, a revelation, and a presentation of how God's creation is meant to be when it's working right (like it had been working in Eden before the fall). In the story of the fall, God had not stopped Loving the world after Adam and Eve left Eden. That great Love has been there all the time. Instances of Love and faithfulness fill the Old Testament as God works to bring human life back to life as God created it in the beginning.

The life and death and resurrection of Jesus are God's work of making visible the supreme truth about life, our great "aha" moment when we can finally see how God created the world to be from the beginning; how it is a world filled to overflowing with unconditional Love, revealing the Love beyond which there is none greater. This greatest Love is the defining center around which all Love, Loving, and being Loved circles, from the day after the fall to the present. Our being confronted with this sacrificial giving of one life for another is the moment when the white-hot spark of the Spirit, Love itself, *awakens us* to the power of Love that has been there all along, in all of life, down through the centuries, from the sleep of the old Adam to the presence and the joy of Love itself all around us. The Spirit enables us to grasp that this is "what it's all about." This is what we mean when we say it happens "through Christ." All the joy we feel in exercising Love, Loving-kindness, compassion, forgiveness, care, and all the rest is stirred up by the Spirit at the bright disclosure of Love's presence at the cross. The truth is there, as it has always been there, a part of God's good creation, waiting to be fully seen once more, to be revealed by the power of the Spirit breathing in us. It's like a curtain opening, a light coming on: *this is how life is supposed to be!* This kind of sacrificial Love is what it's like to be in sync with God, in sync with Love and all God wants for us. The Christian story presents the crucifixion, the giving of one's life for another, holding nothing back, as the true and supreme vision of perfect Love, and all the joyful moments of Love we discover and live and offer and receive are a part of that same Love.

When we begin intentionally to live the way of Jesus' life— his Love, sacrifice, justice, kindness, forgiveness—things begin to change in us. It doesn't mean that the only way to be truly Christian is actually to find the opportunity to die for our friends, and then do it. That's what it probably meant to the early Christians who first heard about the crucifixion, who were experiencing persecution and for whom death and the opportunity to die instead of betraying their friends was an immediate possibility. It may have meant that to Martin Luther and many of the reformers. It may have meant that to Dietrich Bonhoeffer. It may have meant that to Martin Luther King Jr. It might have meant that to any number of persons we may have read about or may have known who unselfishly gave their lives that another might live. And it might mean that to one of us at some point, and we need to see that and be ready.

But what it means for us now, every day, is giving our lives to imitating and living the Loving life of Jesus. When we see that giving is better than getting, that sharing is better than hoarding, giving ourselves away is better than building ourselves up, that the one with the most toys doesn't win, that serving is better than being served, that Love is better than hate, then both our hearts and our minds confirm for us the deep joy of the new life that only God, only Love, can give.

It is a new life in the present. It is not something we wait on heaven for. With all the books and articles about what it is like, and how to get there, heaven, the full realization and presence of the new life, has become a distraction for us. Such widespread obsession with it draws our attention from what is truly important in life. In his letter to the Roman church, Paul wrote that he would gladly give up his hope of a place in heaven with Christ if it would enable his fellow Jews would follow Christ.[9] He would give it all up out of Love for them. In this new life, our neighbor, anyone in need, is more important to us than heaven. Heaven is not our goal. Even joy is not our goal (though when Love happens, joy happens). Sacrificial Love is our goal; giving up our lives daily for our neighbor, for all who are in need, is our goal.

We do not, we cannot, create this new life. We cannot achieve it by Loving or orienting our lives around Love. It is not a reward or a deserved result of a good life. It is God's gift, Love's gift. It doesn't depend on our getting the theological words and concepts right, on believing the correct propositions, on being a part of the right religious institution or, for that matter, any religious institution. The pathway becomes clear as we enter into experiences of unselfish Love, Loving sacrificial acts, actually doing Loving things every day, trusting God, trusting Love (by now you know they are the same thing). This is how we need to spend our time. We discover its power as we fully, intentionally begin to embrace and live the kind of life presented in Jesus' life, his teachings, and his sacrificial Loving care for all people. The way opens up clearly the more we do for others in need and the less we arrange life around ourselves. When two or three gather together to share how exciting that life of Love is, a church is born.

We can block it in this life, we can keep Love out, and we can refuse to be a part of Love, at least for the present. Many people do. Many people try to Love, but can't seem to pull it off. Paul makes it clear that this is an old problem: "I do not understand my own

9. Romans 9:3.

actions," he writes, "for I do not do what I want, but I do the very thing I hate."[10] He is, he says, in need of a rescuer. The life of Love is the rescuer. He can't do it himself. No one can. That new life is a gift from God, it is the gift of Love, and as the Spirit awakens us to it at the cross, and as it is embraced and lived, it changes things. Love itself can be blocked in this life, but not forever, for in the end Love will have its way. Struggle as we might, and as we will, this is the Love that will not let us go.

Back in Eden

Despite the striking differences in the resurrection accounts in the four Gospels, there is one uniting point that draws them together. Up until Easter day, his disciples never quite understood who he was and what it all meant. And then, after his death, he was re-united with them, and *they met him*. We Christians don't believe that he was raised from the dead because the disciples said so, nor do we believe it to be true because the pope says so, or Luther, or Calvin, or Wesley, or Billy Graham, or Sweet Daddy Grace (what a guy!), or our preacher, or Mama or Daddy. We affirm the resurrection, the Love that is alive, only when we have *met* him, in the life experiences of Love, in the telling and retelling of the stories and the singing of the songs. The Spirit, the Love that is the authority of the Bible, speaks to us in and through its pages and at times and places of God choosing; and, hearing it, we begin to realize that Love, the most powerful and the most important thing in the world, never ends, cannot die.

The crucifixion and the resurrection together are the only way a story of eternal Love could end, the only way perfect Love could have its way. Like the entire Christian story that has gone on before, and is yet to come, the resurrection is a revelation, an uncovering of something that was already there and always was there. Paul wrote, "Love never ends."[11] Nor does God ever end, for they are one and

10. Romans 7:14–25.

11. 1 Corinthians 13:8.

the same. Our Love for someone close to us who has died does not end at death, although memories fade through the generations; then how much *more* persistent and eternal is the Love of God for that person. Because God is eternal, and Love is eternal, resurrection is the only way this story, our story, could possibly end. Love is not subject to death. Eternal Love, new life with God, transcends death. Nothing can stop it. Not ever. *Love will have its way.*

The resurrection of Jesus is considered by many to be the culmination and the conclusion of the Christian story, to which the story has been aimed all along. Some people believe it was the plan all the time, and that God and Jesus knew about it, and they simply used it to encourage Christian behavior by tapping into the fear of death and the desire of people to live beyond death. Others believe that it is there to show the trust that Jesus had in his Father in order to instill that degree of trust in God in the lives of his followers. Others see it as a reward to Jesus for good and faithful behavior, encouraging us also to do the good things Jesus did, so that we too will be rewarded and experience resurrection and survive death. My experience is that most people view the resurrection as a mixture of these, something that happened as a sequel to the crucifixion, so that after a few obligatory public appearances Jesus can retire to his ancestral home with his Father, maybe take a couple of weeks off, and then do his continuing work from there— a kind of celestial Facebook.

But when you slow down, study deeply, and listen for the Spirit speaking in unexpected ways through the passage, you sometimes discover that there may be another way to understand the resurrection. I believe that, instead of being sequential, the moment of Jesus' death and the resurrection are one unified event. There is no clear literal indication of this in Scripture (and no indication that it is *not* true; nor is this the first time this interpretation has been expressed), but in Luke's version of the crucifixion, when the thief said, "Remember me when you come into your *Kingdom*," Jesus did respond "*Today* you will be with me in paradise."[12] The three-day gap between Good Friday and Easter Morning is a mystery

12. Luke 23:42–43.

that the church throughout its history has tried to fill in various ways. Still, it was Passover, and the memory of that central event of God's providence and deliverance to freedom, had to be fully appreciated to interpret and explain what they would find at the tomb on Sunday morning. Then there is the business of the wine. In the first three Gospels, Jesus offers wine as his blood to his followers, saying, "I will not drink it again until I drink it in the Kingdom of God." The next time the wine appears, Jesus is on the cross; the Love beyond which there is no greater Love was happening.[13] His journey was over, and this part of his life was almost finished. There was nothing more. Since the wine was received by him, we can understand that the Kingdom he was waiting for, to which he had referred during the last supper, had indeed come with that act of supreme Love there on Golgotha.

So rather than the resurrection being a reward for the sacrifice, rather than the resurrection as a separate event following the crucifixion, later, on Sunday morning, I believe the Spirit is perhaps leading us to understand that Jesus' death and resurrection happen at once, together, at the cross. Jesus' act of sacrificial Love beyond which there is no greater Love, *becomes* resurrection to new life. That life of Love is what resurrection *is*. It *defines* resurrection. Resurrection is the perfect life of Love God created in the beginning in Eden—without death—the kind of life God intended humankind to live, the life God wants for all of us, a kind of restoration of Eden.

That new life that God intends for us, then, is what we catch a glimpse of, by the Spirit touching our hearts, when Love in any of its faces is intentionally put into practice. The resurrection Kingdom is discovered when you give yourself away totally, fully, holding nothing back, for your friends. The Kingdom of Love, of God, comes when we give a cup of cold water to a thirsty person. The Kingdom of new life comes when we forgive and Love our enemies or build just, fair, Loving constructs in the world. The Kingdom of Heaven comes when I put my neighbor's good above my own, and when we establish circumstances of compassion, forgiveness,

13. Mark 15:36–37, but more graphic in John 19:28–30.

healing, and Loving-kindness throughout all the nations. The Kingdom of God's presence comes when we Love sacrificially, expecting nothing in return, experiencing a new life and a new joy simply in the act of Loving. In a single instant, the sacrificial Love enacted at Golgotha and the new life of the resurrection merge, and become one.

In the death of Jesus, perfect Love merges with perfect Love. The Hindu expression of one drop of water (in the case of Jesus, perfectly clean) merging into an ocean (perfectly clean) is a helpful image. The moment the drop of water touches the ocean is both the moment of death and the moment of resurrection and perfection. Our death is much the same, but imperfect, in need of the cleansing ocean, but fully absorbed into it along with all humanity, all creation.

The crucifixion/resurrection, and the Loving promise surrounding our death, foreshadows the story's further conclusion. The early Christian writers' experience of the Spirit couldn't conceive of life's ongoing joys and struggles eternally outside God's created perfection of the life in Eden, and wrote of God's final resolution of the long journey of human life. The Spirit speaks to us through this part of the drama too. In time to come, a time that only God knows, the story will be perfectly concluded, God will gather all people back, and make everything right, and all creation will be together in the new life of perfect Love as the garden was meant to be in the beginning.

There is a danger in this part of the story. It is easy to get so wrapped up in the biblical storyline that we miss the voice of the Spirit speaking through it. The time of God's resolution won't begin in Hollywood style with the destruction of the earth by a huge meteor, the sun's flameout, a life-ending plague, or some kind of environmental catastrophe. These are scientific propositions, and if you try to somehow link and solve the Christian story with them, you will miss the point of the story, what the Spirit has to say. We also get wrapped up in questions like "When will it happen?," "What will it look like?," "What do I have to do to get there?," and

"Who goes and who stays?" These concerns become self-centered distractions from a sacrificial life in the Spirit.

The point of the Christian faith is not "What comes next?" but "Love your neighbor." It is the life of Love in all its forms and faces, giving ourselves totally to the welfare of our neighbor, which is the fulfillment and joy of human life. The Word of the Spirit in this part of the story is that in life and in death, and beyond all that we know, God's hand surrounds us with Love and Loving care that are eternal. (The rest—heaven and all that—is providentially settled. But we'll get to that later).

So, my friend (as the preacher in me takes over, as if he hasn't already), the Christian story means that if you really want to get your life together, don't just look for a study group or a sermon or a book of theology—even this one—and stop worrying about what's going to happen to you at the end of your life. Instead, significantly sacrifice your time and energy and resources and go serve food at a soup kitchen, buy some blankets and take them to some people living on the street, take an afternoon to visit a nursing home resident who has no other visitors. Help build a house for someone who otherwise wouldn't have one. Organize a financial support system for an orphanage or a clinic in India or Africa or the U.S., or anywhere there are children who have no place to go. Join a group working for justice and economic fairness for the poor and those at the margins of society. Go cut the yard for somebody who is too ill to do it, give somebody a ride, visit somebody in prison, buy lunch for somebody who doesn't get out much, or take some kids fishing. These are enough to get you going in the right direction. The Spirit of God (i.e., the Spirit of Love) is waiting for you there with the revelation of a new life in which you begin to move more and more into the loving, majestic life patterns God is trying to knit into you. This kind of life, these experiences of giving your life to another rather than simply possessing it, are what Christians actually mean when they say "Follow Jesus." This new life is the ongoing narrative of the Christian faith, and how its people enter into its story, and celebrate it so that it becomes their own.

8

When Love Seems Lost

And the reality of goblins

God's Answer

IT IS ONE BRIGHT morning in the fall, the week of Halloween. Our four-year-old son and I are on the front porch, waiting for his carpool to the school he attends a couple of mornings a week. It's a beautiful morning, not too cool, just a slight breeze, and I'm working on my second cup of coffee. He waves to his sister and his mother, and watches them as they drive away out of sight headed for her school.

Then he says to me, "Daddy, if mommies and daddies weren't here, would God take care of us?"

I'm not ready for this conversation this early on a Monday morning, but I say, "Yes he would, son. In fact he's taking care of us right now, every day, and all the time. But don't worry; your Mommy and Daddy aren't going anywhere. We'll always take care of you."

He's on my lap, but he turns and looks at me for a moment. "Daddy," he says, "why did God make skeletons and witches and ghosts and goblins?"

"I'm not sure, son, but I think maybe they're mostly just things in stories." (What was I thinking? Did I really think I could get away with that?)

He looks at me and his eyes are like big blue searchlights, and he is absolutely serious. "No!" he says, "They're *real!*"

Already, he knows, he suspects, that not everything in life is good and safe.

God wants for us lives oriented around the secure Love that is God, the Love that is unconditional, universal, never-ending, forgiving, reconciling, the Love that yields care, justice, healing, and joy. A benevolent, trustworthy God, an ever-present Love, wants good things in life *for* us, but it is clear that there are elements in life that God does *not* want for us as well. They are not good, and as our son rightly reminded me, they are real! The God who Loves us, who *is* Love, does not want pain for us, or loneliness or hopelessness. A world in which Love is the most important element does not accept hunger or poverty or want or oppression or lives poisoned with hatred, danger, jealousy, and dark depression. God does not want sickness for us, or tragedy, or house fires or automobile accidents or plane crashes, or senseless random disasters, or death. God does not want the worship of wealth, which saps meaning and happiness and fulfillment in life. God does not want for us the selfish power that destroys community and care. God does not want injustice for us, or unfairness, or for the wrong to overcome the right. God does not want fear and aimlessness and sorrow before the challenges of life, or lonely isolation far from home, far from the Loving center of life. These are all components of life *outside* the garden, where Love often seems lost.

Why then would God, who wants good for us, not fix things? Why not just go ahead and transcend the brokenness of this world, the post-Eden kind of life around us, and bring into creation the good that God wants for us? Why does God allow the evil in this world to go on and on—both the evil in the natural world like floods, earthquakes, and fires, and the evil for which we ourselves must take responsibility? Why would God allow one child to miraculously survive an accident, and yet allow another child on the next block or the next continent to die of cancer, when prayers were lifted for both? Parents know they can't always control things that happen to children. They want to save their children from falling off their tricycles and cracking their tiny heads on a curb, with the devastating damage it could do. They want to save their babies from birth defects and birth accidents. They want to save their children from becoming the bully that pushes a small child off a swing. They want to save children from the tragedy of addiction, and from the terror of arrest and imprisonment for a crime. They never want to hear the phone ring in the middle of the night to hear a voice telling them of an automobile accident. All of us, whether or not you have children of your own, have experienced some such nightmare—the blind, random, purposeless evil that does nothing but hurt and kill, and leave in its wake grief, tears, and fists lifted to heaven in rage. We do what we can, but we can't control the evil that threatens us and our children and all God's people. Think how much parents Love their children, and how much safety, goodness, and full lives we want for them. How much more then, said Jesus, will God fill our lives with good things?[1] Why, then, does God not now act for us all, right now, and overcome our suffering? Can God who is *our* father, *our* mother, not control what happens to *us*?

Some have said that evil is the way God tests us, to see how faithful we are. Some have said that evil happenings are a result of sin, and we deserve what we get. Some have said that God has given us free will so that we bring it on ourselves. Some have said that God allows evil to happen because God is the only one who sees the big picture. I have heard numerous times at funerals the claim that God allowed a child to die now because God knew that later in his life he or she would get cancer and die a painful death. Some have said that God simply is not powerful enough to stop evil, that God is much too busy to cover all the evil things happening in the world, and must just let some of it go by, or that we don't believe the right things, or just didn't pray enough or the right way.

All of these are sad, insensitive, misguided, and unsuccessful attempts to answer the question of evil. They are totally at variance with, and do not take seriously, God's unconditional Love for this world and its people, and they too easily dismiss the powerful

1. Matthew 7:11.

providence of God and the sure promises given to humankind about all the Love that God wants for us, the Love that God is. It is true that God's power and God's Love seem to be at odds with each other. We can affirm God's universal and eternal *Love* for us as the cornerstone of the Christian faith. The same is true of God's *power* in this world and throughout the universe. We simply are not able to put them together before the awful reality of evil, until we finally realize that Love *is* God's power.

Sure, it would be wonderful if God would fix this creation, make everything right and good and joyful and just and true by the end of the week. The church has always affirmed that this will happen, at some unknown time in the future, and a full reconciliation and new creation will come into full existence. This expectation has always been a part of the story.

But it hasn't happened yet. And we live in the present, not in the future. Down through the history of most religions, whenever life in the present has been hard or unbearably painful, there has always been an intense emphasis on looking ahead to the future, which, it is hoped, will be better. This happens periodically in the Christian faith, when a singular obsession with the end of the world, and what must be done to get out of here and off to heaven, begins to emerge. This has the danger of becoming a private selfish quest: I try to figure out how to avoid death or at least to survive it, and accumulate for myself a happy life in heaven, rather than living the life of Jesus, *giving up* my life for my neighbor, affirming that "No one has greater Love than this, to lay down one's life for one's friends."[2]

In the Christian narratives, evil in the world seems to result from the disobedience of Adam and Eve and their discharge from the perfection of Eden , and has infected and corrupted us all. In other words, it is just there, just a part of the life we live, and has been since the beginning. One of the best of the Bible's responses to the problem of evil is the story of God and Job. Job and his friends had argued about why God would allow bad things to happen, and whether or not the evil that appeared in Job's life was punishment,

2. John 15:13

and resulted from something Job did to deserve it. Finally in chapter 38,[3] God answers Job from the whirlwind (the wild stirring up of the Spirit, the breath of God) and takes his and our breath away. Essentially, God says, "There are a lot of things you don't know about me and the way the world works; I am in charge, and things happen in this world beyond your understanding. You cannot know why some things happen and some things do not, nor how they happen. Many things are beyond your comprehension."And then in chapter 42, after being totally put in his place in some of the most beautiful poetry in any language, Job's incredible statement to God is the only one he can make, and the only one we can make: "I know that you can do all things, and that no purpose of yours can be thwarted."[4] In other words, the world is not random. It proceeds according to God's care. It has a loving direction. It has purpose. It is under control. I will still trust you.

What is God's purpose that cannot be thwarted? It is Love. It is fairness, kindness, justice, healing, support, care, and new life, for this is what Love is in our lives. *Love is God's power*, and flows from God, and is God here now, as I write this. It always has been and always will be with us. *And although we cannot fully understand God, and why things happen as they do, we understand and experience Love's power, which is what we truly and urgently need.*

Love is here when friends gather with those who grieve the death of a child, or when a friend brings a meal to one who is injured and unable to function, or when someone sits with you and listens to you without judging you in a time of stress or depression or loss or guilt. Love is here in a phone call just to be in touch, or an email that sends a supporting thought. It is here when a group of women gather, as a mission of their church and community, to create and finance a children's home for kids living on the streets alone, or when Christians travel to lands far away, as a part of their congregation's mission, to provide water purification systems and resources in places of need around the world. That Love is here when one woman takes it on herself to lead her fellow Christians

3. Job 38–41.
4. Job 42:2.

in establishing what became the largest operation of its kind in the U.S., providing a site in her church so that people in and beyond the membership could purchase coffee from small low-income farmers around the world, enabling needed income and jobs.

God's answer to evil is not explanations. God's answer is Love, and Love has not deserted us, as painful and unjust as our daily experience may often be. It is that Love, that presence and power of God, on which we lean, right now, today, tonight, in the middle of evil. It is a gift; it cannot be purchased, nor can it be lost. It can be blocked to some extent, at least in the present, by people who have no wish to be a part of it, or who are so lost or hurting that they cannot see it. But it's always there. When you experience Love before evil's frightening presence, you experience God's power.

Throughout the Bible, Love as God's answer to evil is often presented not as an immediate fix, but as evolving, often agonizingly gradual, but always moving forward toward full expression. The Bible's story is linear, moving in a direction toward what is expressed as the final rule of God, the full and perfect presence of Love in creation, and along the way the brilliance of that new creation breaks into life from time to time with surprising and welcome joy. In Romans 8:28, Paul writes of the way that is happening and how Love and evil interact in the meantime. This passage has become a popular reference presenting the unfailing Love and power of God, but its wide varieties of translations are significant. Here is how the majority of translators have rendered this passage: "*We know that all things work together for good for those who love God, who are called according to his purpose.*"[5]

There are two reasons I have felt the Spirit nudging me to a deeper more detailed study of this passage, an urging that yields a different word from this passage for me. First, as I try to listen for God's Loving power in the passage, the phrase "All things work together for good" doesn't ring true. All things *don't* work together for good. On a rainy day, the road was slick, the truck had bald tires, the driver was drinking, and the truck slid into the children waiting for a school bus. All things—the tires, the slick road, the

5. NRSV.

drinking driver—certainly didn't work together then for a good outcome, at least as far as we can tell.

But the structure of the Greek sentence here lends itself to a different wording, a different ordering of the components of the line, used in a number of New Testament translations,[6] with the possible, even likely phrase: *"In all things, God works for good."* Love, caring, support, and weeping with those who weep are all part of God's "working for good," in a world that is sometimes truly tragic. God's answer to these events isn't explanations; it is Love.

Second, the phrase indicates that God's Love is *"for* those who love God, who are called" by God. Apparently, all others are on their own. The Greek word translated as "for," however, is actually better translated elsewhere in the New Testament, as "to," so that it reads, *"to* those who Love God" and feel the call of God. That is, *to* those who are involved in Love and Loving-kindness in their lives, to them it is very clear how God is working for good through them and their Loving service, even in the face of evil.[7]

So here is my loose but, I believe, literal translation in which I believe the Spirit opens up a deeper understanding of the passage:

> *"We know that to those who experience the Love of God, who are filled with yearning for that Love to guide and complete their lives and all of life—to them it is clear that in all of life's moments, events, and people, God is working for good."*

Or perhaps:

> *"We know that those who engage in intentional Loving-kindness, who have already felt the joy according to the purposes of Love, can see how Love works in all things for good."*

God is Love, and the way a person loves God, Loves and follows Jesus, and lives the life of the Spirit is by patiently living the powerful presence of Love every day. Quick fixes are rare, but the movement

6. See for example Romans 8:28, RSV.

7. See 1 Corinthians 1:18 for similar use of the same word.

toward good is ongoing, God is working his purpose out, and Love will have its way.

When evil appears in life, the answer to it, the resolution of it, is not to figure out why it happened, or why God "allowed" it to happen. The resolution of evil, and evil events in life, is Love, and Loving action by God's people "in all things." This is what God does for and with all of us. This is the presence of God as Love with all.

Our struggle with evil in the world is strengthened and encouraged in the certainty that God is still the master of the universe and will bring Love to full fruition in "the fullness of time." "God with us" doesn't mean that we have to do our part equal to God's part or it doesn't get done. We are not co-creators, we are not equal to God; we are stewards, servants, underlings, children. The Love of a present God is so much greater than our small efforts. God calls us and uses us for holy work, and strengthens us for that work. But lest we think more highly of ourselves than we should, it isn't as if God has no hands but ours. God is not limited by what our hands decide to do or do not do. We don't have that kind of power. God simply wants us to be committed instruments of that Love, and for our hands to be busy for the sake of those we serve for their release from whatever powers are separating them from full, Loving lives. When we and those we serve live fully immersed in a Loving lifestyle, we are in constant communion with God. God is working through events both good and bad, and through people who are good and bad, to bring about a new and holy history. We do not and cannot claim to fully understand all that happens in the world, and sometimes our patience wears thin, but we affirm that God is in control.

In all things, in all events, in all tragedies, in all fears, in all pain, it is not our belief of what is true or not true, not correct doctrine, not always knowing the right things to say or not say; rather, it is the power of Love given into our hands and hearts, the power of a trustworthy God who heals and renews, who gets us through the hard times, and creates all around us from time to time glimpses of the brilliant light of new life and perfect Love, working in all things together toward a final pattern for good.

God's answer to evil is not explanations. God's answer to evil is Love.

The Path of Suffering

The Christian church understands that there is another element of our dealing with evil: the reality and the role of suffering.

In the church's story from its earliest days, suffering has always been a part of the Christian discipline. Suffering and evil in the New Testament church often took the form of persecution by official political powers. Today that kind of persecution still exists in Christian communities across the globe, and however we can, we join their struggle. Hurt and sadness and injustice are real wherever and however they appear. Whenever anyone anywhere suffers for any reason, we all suffer. When anyone is hungry, we all are hungry. When anyone is lonely, we all are lonely. This means that we don't always live superficially happy, bright, and smiling lives, constantly cheerful, delivered from the pain of the world. Their suffering is ours.

But we don't walk around with perpetual frowns for what a painful and sin-filled world we live in. We take seriously the world around us as it is, respond to it as servants, and constantly celebrate the presence of God and the power of Love, with great joy. Remembering and being awakened and ignited by the cross, and the perfect Love that happened there, we willingly and confidently join the journey and the music of Love.

In his suffering, Jesus took everything the world could throw at him as he exhibited the Love beyond which there was is no greater Love. The result was pain and death, but it was also the assurance of God's presence, and the visible continuation of Love beyond this life. When Jesus held out his hands and showed his side to the apostles, he was saying, "This is what I want for you" (not *from* you, *for* you). It is not just to suffer for the sake of suffering or because God is some kind of sadist who enjoys seeing people suffer. God wants for us the experience of courageous faithfulness to our calling to live out the Love that the Spirit awakens in us, the Love that is God, and to take everything the world and its powers of evil throw at us that would "threaten to undo us."[8] In times of suffering and pain, God wants for us to know the joy of not just enduring, but prevailing in the powerful providence of God, the certain power of Love, in the full awareness that God is still with us, and that the eternal purposes of God, the eternal purposes and patterns of Love, are being put together every hour.

The life you discover God wants for you means putting the concerns of others *above* your own—feeding the hungry, lifting up the poor, welcoming the outcast, and sacrificially giving your life to your friends. This life takes Love when it is not returned, it takes sacrifice when no one will know, it takes patience when things refuse to happen, it takes assertiveness when aggressiveness is easier (and more fun), it takes forgiveness when it is not deserved, and it takes life when it seems that death is everywhere. It is affirming the countless gifts of Love as the most important things in the world. God is not against you. God is not playing games with you or messing with your head. You can't buy God off if only you can find the right price. God is already *for* you, always has been, and has wonderful free gifts of Love for you.

Do not be afraid, says Jesus. Suffer with me when it is necessary. It is an experience not to be missed. Do not be afraid of evil. Overcome evil with good. The pattern of perfect Love is coming together. Take all the world throws at you, certain that Love, peace, a full life, and resurrection are also what I want for you. Love your neighbor, Jesus says, and die for your friends. This is not what God wants *from* you; this is what God wants *for* you!

The Constant Presence of Prayer

In times of evil, pain, and suffering, as well as joy and thanksgiving, we hold on to prayer. We know we can't have a conversation

---

8. Presbyterian Church (U.S.A.), *Presbyterian Hymnal*, 260.

with God in the same way we can with each other. The Spirit, in breathing into the church's language, has opened up for us a point of contact with God, with Love itself—the Loving, powerful, creative center of the universe—with words and images so that we experience "someone to talk to" despite our human limitations that keep us from a full understanding of God. How does that work? How can that be?

The apostle Paul writes that in fact we can't pray as we might want to, but the Spirit prays in us, with "sighs too deep for words."[9] Prayer is not just something that we do or say. Prayer is something that God does in us, that Love does in us, in a constant, ongoing presence, as the Spirit of God breathes prayer in us. Prayer doesn't happen just when we consciously pray. It is true that we often close our eyes and bow our heads and speak words to God, but these are the outward symbols of true prayer, the beginnings of prayer, an attempt to enter into true prayer. For just like other gifts from God, prayer is a result of God's grace, God's Love alone, which wells up in us.

There is behind and in every prayer we speak a sigh that is deeper than the words we use. It's a sigh that at once expresses the depth of our feelings and our deepest yearnings. It's the Spirit of God who forms these sighs in us, for us, who actually transforms our spoken prayers so that the prayer that is lifted to God is the deep, truthful, wordless Loving sigh that is really in our hearts all along. We cannot pray, so God initiates and forms the prayer itself. Prayer is part of the free gift of God's grace, and not of our own doing.

This is why there are times when our prayers don't seem to be answered, for it is not the spoken prayers, the words *we* use, but the sighs that come from deep inside us, which the Spirit forms, that God answers, the prayers for which Love is often the answer—an answer that is often quite different from the one we thought we wanted to hear. The spoken prayers become only the way, the first step, to God's presence. It's as if God is listening, and says, "This— the contents of this wordless sigh—is what you really mean to pray about, this is what is really in your heart, and I hear you, and I Love

9. Romans 8:26.

you. My answer to you is, 'I Love you. I am with you.'"God answers the sighs that we sometimes don't know are in us. *God answers not our words, God answers us,* the undiscovered sighs deep inside us, with Loving presence and Loving purposes for each of us and for all creation. These are the answers not always to our words, but to our prayers that come from the deepest corners of our hearts. This is the kind of prayer God wants *for* us. This is the kind of communion that God gives, that Love provides. This is the kind of prayer experience that is truly powerful, life-giving, and life-changing.

We inadvertently like to take credit for prayer. We speak of the power of prayer, the ways in which prayer "works." I remember an incident in which a small child was dying of cancer, and people set up a schedule of prayers, each person praying for fifteen minutes, and then the next person on the list would take over for the next assigned fifteen minutes, day and night, as if to persuade God to save this child. The child died, and one of the leaders of the prayer chain said, "Perhaps if only we had just one or two more people praying, or if we had each person pray for thirty minutes instead of fifteen, it would have been different." Such compassion is laudable, and is certainly the depth of Love Christians are called extend. But that approach to prayer assumes the power of the people praying, and the power of their prayers, instead of the power of God. It presents prayer as a tool that we use to get what we want from a God who perhaps doesn't really want to give it, but might if we pestered God enough.

But it is not ever the power of prayer we seek; it is always and only the power of God, the power of Love. We would Love to have that kind of power, a kind of veto over what God is doing in the world that doesn't seem right to us, the power to direct God's attention to certain circumstances we find important but which we feel God may have missed, the power to make things happen. But we do not have it. God is not waiting for our direction on what to do in any given situation. God already knows how providence is unfolding. This is not to say that we shouldn't pray for what we want, and what we believe is right, and what we believe should happen. Certainly we should pray for persons to be healed, to be set free, to find peace in their lives, to end loneliness and fear, for an end to war and violence, and all the other heaviness that is in our hearts in the face of evil in the world. We should pray for rain for dry fields, and for the land to be delivered from floods, and even for Congress (especially for Congress). Certainly we should pray to God about the joys and burdens of our own lives. God already knows what we want to say, and we are not fooling God when we don't say exactly what is on our minds and in our hearts.

But Love itself is already at work among us in the loving people who surround us, and they are God's voice, and, in many real, visible, substantive ways, God's answers to prayer. An elderly woman told me about hearing from her son that her granddaughter had been hit by a truck as she ran out into the street, and was hospitalized in critical condition. She spent the morning frantically waiting to hear from someone from the hospital, not knowing, and waiting for God's answer to her prayers asking why such a thing would happen. She was raging, pleading, demanding an answer; she said she supposed she was waiting for some kind of voice from heaven. Before long, her friends started coming over with time to talk and listen. One of them was a nurse, who called a friend at the hospital and was able to answer her questions about her granddaughter's condition. Over the next few days, by simply being there with her, they became the faces, the practitioners of Love in many different ways. This Love, rather than some cosmic theory about why tragedy happens, or a dramatic supernatural intervention, was God present in Love, answering her prayers. It's not just you and Jesus all alone. God's Loving voice is waiting to be spoken and heard all around you.

In the Gospels, Jesus' disciples came running up to him one day and said, "In case you haven't noticed, we've got five thousand hungry people sitting here. We've got to tell them to go start looking for some food." But Jesus said, "*You* give them something to eat."[10] This is where God is at work. This is where God's loving voice is heard. This is how prayers are answered. *You* give them something to eat.

10. Mark 6:30–44.

Late one winter afternoon, when our little girl was small, maybe four or five years old, I had just come home and was relaxing on the couch with the evening paper. It had slipped my mind that when you have children you have to be ready for anything. She came out from her bedroom, after her bath, all clean and smelling of powder, in her pajamas and bathrobe, beautiful even then, but this day sobbing as if her heart would surely break. She came over to where I was sitting and, sobbing so that she could barely get the words out, cried out to me, "Daddy, I don't want to die!!" (I don't remember, if I ever knew, what triggered this in her, but it was an exact picture of how we bring our prayers to God.) I took her on my lap and held her and rocked her, and she cried it out. Looking back, I don't remember what I said—probably that she wasn't going to die for a long time, and sometimes people die, and God takes care of us even when we die, and we'll always be together, and on and on. I really don't know if the answers were good or theologically correct, and I don't think anything I said made much difference, for what I really wanted was for her to feel my Love for her and my faithfulness to her, and I wanted to set her troubled heart at rest.[11]

Now, if I Love my child as much and as fully as I can, as imperfectly as that may be, and try as hard as I can to listen to her and answer her tears and the deep unnamed sigh that was in her (although she named it pretty well, as children are able to do), think how much *more* God will listen to *us*. Imagine how much *more* God will help *us* form our prayers, and hear them, and answer *us* and the sighs inside *us* that are too deep for words, the prayers that struggle to find words. God's answering, if we will listen for it, is Love's strong arm around our shoulders.[12] This loving answer is often provided by someone who will sit and listen, or bring a meal over to a grieving family, or stay by a hospital bed, or who will lend a hand when it is needed. Prayer is like a weeping child climbing onto her father's or mother's lap, being held, and being listened to

11. See John 14:1, NEB.

12 See Luke 11:11–13.

even when nobody is quite sure of what to say. Love's presence is God's answer.

Despite occasional feelings to the contrary, Love is never lost. Sometimes it is mislaid, or hidden, but it can be rediscovered. For some it can be found in music, or drama, or painting, or another of the arts. For some it is in a time of prayer or meditation, reading, or silence. For some it is found in a comfortable porch rocker, a light warm summer breeze, and a Bible. For some it is found in a walk in the winter woods, or in the sudden discovery of a mathematical formula, or in a symphony. For most—ultimately for all—it can always be found where people gather to share Loving-kindness and caring spirits, and listening ears, and an eagerness to put oneself aside and be a servant where the need is great. Love is not lost. It's right there. It will always be there. It will not let us go. That's why it's known as good news.

9

The Final Universal Gift

"Love never ends"[1]

I BELIEVE THAT ONE of the greatest dangers in any Christian congregation or church organization is the way it deals with the concept of heaven and the whole idea of life after death. It is a danger because it can lead to a very selfish faith, something we want individually for ourselves, a desire for personal comfort and happiness after death, which gets all hung up with what one has to do to achieve it. It is also a danger because it distracts us from the true purpose and goal of the faith, which is *not* "to go to heaven when we die," but to engage in sacrificial Love for our neighbors, without worrying or even considering whether or not we will get anything (like heaven) from it. I realize and affirm that the assurance of the life beyond this life is a great comfort when life begins to draw toward its ending, or in moments of tragedy and death. I have seen it many times and I believe in it, but it can never be the primary goal of the Christian faith. Sacrificial Love, Loving-kindness, justice, forgiveness, all these and more are, together, our goal.

So it is with some uncertainty that I spend time writing these pages about something I don't think we ought to spend a lot of time thinking about. But what I want to do here is focus on the foundation for the assurance that sets us free from having to worry about heaven and whether or not we will "make it," so that we can

1. 1 Corinthians 13:8.

be more at work doing what we are to do and being who we are supposed to be. Eternal life with God is an unachievable gift, just as creation, and life itself, are gifts. That new life beyond life is already solidly established, so that we can turn loose of uncertainty and confusion and fear. We can stop worrying. Just as God has always been "for" us, so God will continue to be for us beyond the conclusion of this life. That is why this statement is true for us all: "In life and in death, we belong to God."[2]

In almost fifty years of officiating at well over a thousand funerals and memorial services, I have never once come across family members who assume or seriously assert that the one who has died has gone to a fiery hell. I'm sure others in other church traditions have, but I have not. They may have thought it, and I'm reasonably sure they did. They may even have affirmed it out loud to each other. But when they come together to say the final words and lift up the final prayers, they seemed to believe, or at least hope, that somehow death results in being with God, and that somehow God will make things right, things that were so wrong in this world. I have also never seen a printed obituary or other death notification that indicate anything other than the deceased has "gone to the breast of Jesus" or "has flown away to be in the arms of God" or has "left this world to be welcomed by the angels [or other specific deceased family members] at the gates of heaven." It's either that, or they remain silent on any expected future residence. The closest I ever came was after the graveside service of a ninety-year-old rural farmer with an apparently well-deserved reputation for pure meanness. I overheard a local banker say to an elderly neighbor of the deceased, "Well, I guess he's with the angels now." The neighbor rolled a cigar around in his mouth, thought a minute, and replied, "Well, I don' know. I got a baaad feelin' 'bout that boy."

Certainly there are many churches of various kinds that have those same feelings. These churches believe that some people go to a place called "heaven" and others to a place called "hell" when they die, and claim to be able to identify which are which. I'm sure

---

2. Presbyterian Church (U.S.A.), *Book of Confessions*, 341.

that the families they have talked with may well have affirmed the deceased's place in the great congregation of the punished. But although 74 percent of the American population seems to believe that a heavenly reward waits for those who have lived a good and ethical life (and have therefore earned it and will probably file suit if they don't get it), and 57 percent believe in the reality of hell for those who don't behave,[3] I sense a kind of deep uneasiness, even resistance, in people in general to the concept of a God who Loves us but allows a person who has died to be eternally and irrevocably lost in torture and punishment as a result of an unacceptable life performance.

Some kind of life after this one has always been a part of the Christian faith, although there is general disagreement about what it will be like. What does God want for us at the end of life as we know it? Where does God's grace lead us? Does Love as God's presence extend to all of us or just some of us (or, perhaps, any of us) beyond life as we know it? If you are looking for a clear written answer, the Bible seems to be of two minds on this.

There are a number of passages indicating that, at least for some, there exists the danger of an eternal punishment either at the end of life as we know it or beginning in the present and extending beyond this life. In our culture, much of what is pictured as eternal punishment comes from much later writers, such as Dante in the fourteenth century and John Milton in the seventeenth century, and many others; but it is clearly a part of biblical literature. In Mark's Gospel the fire is unquenchable, ongoing, and eternal, so it doesn't end with non-existence, but continues indefinitely with pain.[4] In John's vision of the new creation, he writes of torment and smoke of fire that goes up forever.[5] The author of 2 Thessalonians writes that the coming Lord Jesus will inflict vengeance on those who do not know God and on those who do not obey the gospel of our Lord Jesus, and they will suffer the punishment of eternal destruction,

3. Pew Forum, "U.S. Religious Landscape Survey: Religious Beliefs and Practices Key Findings," 10.

4. Mark 9:43.

5. Revelation 14:11; 19:3; 20:10.

separated from the presence of the Lord.[6] But the passage most often cited as illustrative of this theme in the Bible is in Matthew, when Jesus speaks of all the nations (that is, the Gentiles, everyone, sometimes including the Jews) being separated into the saved and the unsaved on the basis of whether or not they gave food to the hungry and water to the thirsty, or clothes to the naked, or visited those in prison, or welcomed the stranger. Those who fail this test are sent away into eternal punishment, the fire prepared for the devil and his angels. Those who pass it achieve eternal life with God.[7]

The theme that seems to be presented in these passages indicates that the eternal destiny of human beings is determined by what they have done or not done, on the basis of belief or unbelief, or on the basis of a Calvinistic choice made by God before the beginning of creation. A significant number of Christians and non-Christians interpret the Bible and the Christian faith this way. What it means for them is that, according to the order God has put together, some or many or perhaps most people will not be welcomed into the heavenly kingdom of God. They will either be in eternal punishment and pain or they will be discarded, will perish, and will no longer exist.

Alongside this view of eternal punishment, eternal death, and ceasing to exist, there seems to be another. It contends that God's will is that all persons, created and loved by God, will be forgiven, reconciled, recreated, remade, received, made new beyond death, and shall live forever in the heavenly kingdom beyond life as we now know it.

The initial affirmation of this theme is found early, as noted before in Genesis, when God chooses Abram to extend the blessing God to the world. In you, God says to Abram, *all* the families of the earth *shall* be a part of the "blessing!"[8] We find those same echoes in Psalm 22: "*all* the ends of the earth shall remember and turn to the Lord; and *all* the families of the nations shall worship

6. 2Thesssalonians 1:6–8.

7. Matthew 25:31–46.

8. Genesis 12:1–2.

before him."[9] In Ephesians, God's plan set forth in Christ is to gather up *all* things in him . . ."[10] In Paul's first letter to Timothy, it is God's desire that *everyone* be saved and come to the knowledge of the truth through Christ Jesus.[11] In 1 John, the writer states that Jesus "is the atoning sacrifice for our sins, and not for ours only but also for the sins of the *whole* world."[12] In Paul's first Corinthian letter, Paul affirms that just as all die "in" Adam, so *all* will be made alive "in" Christ.[13] We didn't have an option to being in Adam; we just are. In the same way, says the passage, we have no option to being in Christ. God has already indicated here that all will be in Christ. We have access in the present to the discovery of God's grace "through Christ"[14]; that is, we discover it by living the life of Love as Jesus lived, the highest form of which was his death on the cross. Even in our weakness and failure, God's Love is constant, for "God has imprisoned all in disobedience so that he may be merciful to *all*."[15] It's done. The sacrificial death of Jesus was a total revealing of what God's Love looks like, for *all*, for the world.

Clearly, there seems to be two distinct, conflicting themes that find their way through the Old and New Testaments. One says that the participation of humankind in the kingdom of God after the life we know is not for all, and that achieving and arriving at the new life after death depends on how one lives this life, or what one's system of belief or devotion is. The other says that grace is absolute, that we can do nothing to deserve the new life in the kingdom of God, and that all persons are to be forgiven, made new (different, better, corrected, made righteous from their former sinful selves), and brought into the new life now and beyond death. One says my salvation, my future in this life and beyond, depends on me,

9. Psalm 22:27.
10. Ephesians 1:10.
11. 1 Timothy 2:4.
12. 1 John 2:2.
13 1 Corinthians 15:22.
14. Romans 5:2.
15. Romans 11:32.

and what I do or don't do. The other says my salvation—my life—depends on God alone.

What do we do about these two divergent views of Christian belief? We could count up the number of passages of Scripture that spring from each view, and then declare that our theology will be the view that has more passages in its corner. But what then to do with the other view, still there in Scripture? Well, we could do what is basically done now. Each side could interpret the other side's passages in such a way as to support its own view. For example, the passage in Romans, "God has imprisoned all in disobedience so that he may have mercy on all,"[16] could be for all people everywhere, or it could be interpreted as "all Christians," or saying that "he *may* or *might* have mercy on all, but not necessarily, since it depends on what they do to get it" as outlined elsewhere in the New Testament. The Matthew 25 use of the Greek word for "eternal" could mean forever or it could mean for a long but not endless time. But the term "eternal life" and the term "eternal punishment" in the passage employ the same Greek word for *eternal*.[17] Either life with God or life in punishment are both never-ending, or they are both temporary. The few times the word "hell" is used in the New Testament, the Greek word used is almost always "Gehenna,"[18] which is the garbage dump outside Jerusalem's walls, which burned day and night. It could mean that without Love, without Christ, life feels pretty much like a dump of garbage, worthless, filthy, and smelly. The word linguistically could also be used to describe the future of a person's life, in eternal fire after death. The arguments could be never-ending.

It is important to take all of Scripture very seriously, with great care, in trying to answer questions about what the words of the Bible say. But this one sounds like a draw. I don't see how a conclusion can be reached simply by trying to find the right answer in Scripture. There are just too many options.

16. Romans 11:32.
17. Matthew 25:31–46.
18. As in Matthew 5:22.

Some choose another solution, namely that the conflict is truly there between both themes, and that it is all mystery, we cannot understand it, and therefore we must leave it up to the wisdom and the mystery and the mercy of God alone. We simply cannot know. We can only hope for it.

There is indeed much that is mystery in the world and in God's relationship to us. There is indeed much we do not know. We have come across such mystery in considering evil in the world. We cannot always understand the ways of God's love for us. Mystery is a part of the human setting. Trust itself assumes mystery, for if there is no mystery then there is no need for trust, no need for faithfulness. Mystery—not knowing—is part of who we are. Some parts of the Bible present us with mystery we simply cannot grasp. The Bible itself is part of God's revelation to us, and we do not have control on how and when and what God reveals. In our Christian journeys we will always contend with some degree of mystery.

Leaving this whole business in mystery, however, sounds like a dodge. The full extent of grace and Love and God's powerful providence is unresolved and left hanging, if not beaten. The Christian faith is either good news for all, or it is good news for some and bad news for some, or more likely, it is bad news for all. Whichever it is, it should be proclaimed as such.

But the resolution between these two conflicting biblical themes rests not with our finding the right interpretation or the correct linguistic content of the words or the solution to the "right answer" in the written text. As I indicated previously, it is found in our commitment to listening for the Spirit, the voice of God, the voice of Love that *emerges through Scripture, and carries us to a deeper truth and a more profound Love, through the action of the Holy Spirit, into the presence of God's truth.* The Bible requires steady and careful study, but it is not a puzzle to be solved by our skill or intellect. We listen for the Spirit moving in the words of Holy Scripture, and look for the *Loving* presence of God there. Remember, we do not worship the Bible; we worship only God. More important than what the Bible "says" is what God says *through* the Bible.

What we in the church hear, rather than a spirit of vengeance or death, is a Loving Spirit emerging through Scripture and our own life experience of God's Love, leading us to affirm that our destiny at the end of this life is as God has promised; that we, though undeserving, and all creation will be with God, recreated, safely in the presence of perfect Love, perfected eternal life with God, for *all*. What form it takes, no one knows; it is yet to be revealed—a heaven, or a new earthly city, or an experience yet to be defined. Certainly it will not be in terms and constructs we can imagine. We don't have to worry about that. In fact, it becomes an unacceptable distraction if we do. All we can say is that we (all of us) will be with God, embraced in the Love that will not let us go.

The Love the Spirit has revealed to us is bigger than life and death, and never ends. It bears repeating that we know that when someone dear to us dies, the Love we have for that person doesn't die with him or her. That love lives on. If our Love continues (even if our memories begin to fade), think how much *more* Love itself, God present, will never fail to surround those who have died. The Love in which God has established creation is eternal; it is for all creation and all time. Anything less would be an expression of *imperfect* Love. God will not Love all of his creation and all in it, as his children, and then snatch away that Love at death, or any time preceding it. That holy Love has always been there, and has never left God's children in this life, even in the presence of their poor performance, bad behavior, or lack of trust in God. Abandoning them at death, leaving them outside the realm of Love for any reason, would be settling for Love's failure, and God's failure to be able to bring finally to fulfillment the garden-world God always intended. It would be a tragic contradiction to the joy of eternal Love with which the Spirit has filled our hearts and minds.

The certainty of an ongoing life secure beyond this life cannot be attained from the logical reasoning of the mind. Many continue to try to "prove" or "disprove" legalistically or scientifically, or even experientially, the validity of life after death, and what it does or does not look like. But that kind of answer attempts to establish evidence, which is the work of science, and scientific evidence is pretty conclusive that life ends at death, and that there are other likely scientific/physiological origins for supernatural experiences. As real as an experience of heaven or life after death seems to the one recalling it from a near death or other such event, it does not yield a secure foundation of evidence, because, as with other attempts to approach religion scientifically, it is always open to the appearance of future evidence that could discredit it. This does not mean that no one has ever had an accurate experience of life beyond what we know—we cannot limit how God works—it just indicates that it is not indisputable evidence of that new life. Eternal Love, God's presence beyond death, however, is not dependent on scientific, logical proof or the lack of it, nor does it depend on having one's mind changed, being grudgingly "convinced" by irrefutable evidence that Love is in fact eternal. Love is a realization, a discovery that seizes the heart with power and joy. It is a revelation that is uncovered in the common experiences of life rather than in private experiences of only a few, the validity of which is not subject to logical or scientific origins, or evaluation. Its intensity is not subject to proof of some kind that it actually exists. Its source, as expressed in Scripture, is unknowable in any ordinary sense, for "No one has ever seen God. It is God the only son who is close to the Father's heart who has made him known."[19] The presence of Jesus in Scripture and in our experience, the face of Love, the heart of God, is the experience of the breath of perfected Love, of God, breathed into the soul and the heart by the enrichment of the Spirit of God. Proof of its existence is not relevant to the one who experiences it.

The affirmation of this perfected Love emerges from this realization: God, the force and Spirit of Love, is such that it is ongoing, eternal, and will never desert us for any reason. "I will be with you always" means just that. Love will never let any of us go.

Here is a family living in absolute poverty in a housing project in a rundown part of a multi-million population city. Both parents work in low-income jobs, he in a convenience store that is

19. John 1:18.

robbed at gunpoint weekly, and she waiting tables in a bar, both with no benefits and minuscule chance for advancement. The neighborhood is high in crime and dangerous. The drug lords run everything. The apartment has four small rooms and a bathroom in which the plumbing breaks down regularly. The parents love their children, and they try to be good parents. They do all they can for their family, try to live by values of integrity and truth, and sometimes attend a small storefront church in the neighborhood. But still they fear for their children. The oldest, a boy, seventeen, has totally rejected the values of the parents, has been arrested twice, and sometimes doesn't come home at night at all. A daughter, fifteen, is angry, hardly speaks to her parents, and is still in school but has been in trouble with the police for shoplifting. Another son, twelve, hangs out with gang members, skips school regularly, but tries to take care of his younger sister, seven, who has had something happen in her life that she won't talk about and has made her afraid to go outside the apartment, even to school. It's a life of fear and powerlessness and sadness and guilt. One day, unexpectedly, they come into possession of a big house in a small community many miles away, where they are to be provided with good higher paying jobs and opportunities for education, training and advancement, in a safe neighborhood with caring neighbors, a town with a low crime rate, clean air, good schools, and a life filled with new opportunities (There is even a Presbyterian church on the corner!). It is a new life for them, a new life that could remake them all into new people.

The question is:

> Which of their children do you think the parents will take with them? Which of your children would you take?

The answer is, of course, *all of them*. They are their children! Whatever the risks or uncertainties, they will take them all. They brought them into the world. They have cared for them through all the joys and difficulties of growing up. They have never stopped loving them through the fears, the temptations, and the successes and failures of childhood and youth. Irrespective of what they deserve or do not deserve, irrespective of whether their difficulties are the fault of the children or their parents, irrespective of their rebellion and their rejection of their parents, still their parents will take all of them to the new life. In the real world it may work out for them, but it may not. There may be problems with this or that child, but don't miss the point of this tale. Out of the deep Love that these parents obviously have for their children, it is clear that they will love them no matter what happens.

Now, if you multiply the Love that you see in these parents by an infinite number, you will begin to see the magnitude of the Love of the God who is Love for *all* of us. God wants to take us *all* into the new eternal resurrection life, where we *all* will be made new along with the whole creation. The point is not what it will look like. The point is that no one will be left out. *God, Love present, will leave no one behind.* That has been the plan and the intention from the beginning, when God first gave Abram his marching orders: *all* the nations shall receive the blessing, the Love of God. Do we really think anything could interrupt the loving desires of God? We can block the living of the life of Christ in *this* life; we can live as though there were no loving purposes of God. We can live in shallowness and selfishness as if the cross did not exist, and Jesus was a sucker, and sacrificial love was not revealed there at all. But ultimately the power of Love will never be blocked.

One of my favorite Peanuts cartoons shows Lucy looking out the window at the rain, worried about a worldwide flood. Linus, looking very wise, as usual, quotes Genesis 9, where God promised Noah that the flood will never happen again, and that the rainbow is the sign of the promise. Lucy responds, "You've taken a great load off my mind!" Linus responds, "Sound theology has a way of doing that."[20]

The realization of God's universal, eternal Love for all humankind will take a load off a lot of minds. And so it should. It's good news. Sound theology puts Love above any system we can

20. Charles Schultz, *Peanuts*, April 13, 1965, quoted in Grenz and Olson, *Who Needs Theology?*, 134.

extrapolate from Scripture, for there are too many possible systems there to choose from. Because God is Love, all our talk about God (theology) should be about Love, and rather than threats or fear, it should truly take a load off our minds, and give peace to our troubled hearts.[21] Let's keep it simple. God is Love, and Love will never let us go.

So stop being afraid. Stop spending a lot of time worrying about dying and whether or not you'll go to heaven. *Heaven is not your goal. Loving your neighbor is your goal.* The fearful, the lonely, the sick, all those around you in need, are your goal. Put your energy into living the life of Jesus, the life of Love, as a servant to the world here and now. That's the only place you will ever find real joy and real peace! You need to have more concern for your neighbor than heaven. Let heaven go; it's already promised to you, and it's already in place for all of us. You're already eternally Loved. The truly joyful life is in living that Love, and giving it away. That's the kind of life God wants for you. Now!

But wait a minute! If we start proclaiming universal salvation, that beyond this life and death everyone is to join in life together with God in some kind of "paradise," and that this is going to happen to *everyone*, are people then going to simply live any way they please? Will there then be no eternal consequences for actions good or bad? How can that be? We would seem to be saying that it doesn't matter whether you do good or do evil, whether you live by hate or by Love. Come into the faith early, come into the faith late with a deathbed confession, or don't come in at all—the full results are the same for all. Without some kind of pressure, some kind of fear of bad results for bad life performance, why would anyone feel he or she ought to do good at all? We would have chaos. Everyone would do as he or she pleases and nothing more. What would become of the effort to live better, and find new life in Christ? Because we could eternally "get away with it," our infection with sin would rule completely.

21. See John 14:1, NEB.

Imagine for a moment that you have just arrived on a college campus (lucky you) for your first year, ready to begin your studies. You are in your dorm room the night before classes begin, and there is a knock on your door. It's a committee of faculty members and students who inform you that you have been elected to Phi Beta Kappa, the international scholastic honorary society, and they are there to congratulate you. That honor will never be taken away from you, during your college years or beyond. It is yours forever. Now you will do one of two things. You may sleep late the next morning, hardly ever attend classes, barely study at all, float through college and happily attach your Phi Beta Kappa key to your watch chain (if you have one) and your resume. You will stop doing good because you don't have to. Or, on the other hand, you will realize who you are, one who has received a gift you did not deserve, one from whom much is expected, and you will work hard during your college career to live up to the person you have been made into. In so doing, you will discover the joys of all the gifts of learning and growth available to you, and your life will be full and exciting and joyful.

In a world in which universal salvation is embraced by the church, I'm sure some people will live out the gift and the joy of a life of Love and being Loved, a life in God's presence, and some will not, pretty much as they do now. But because the church will have trusted the Loving power of God more than the power of fear, more and more people will be set free from fear, and will be able to embrace and live and celebrate a Loving joyful life in the Spirit. So we invite and encourage the world to join with the church, as part of its institutional forms or beyond them, trusting in intentional Loving-kindness as a way of life, living the life of the servant, structuring life not for ourselves but for the other, the neighbor, even for the enemy, to end hostility in the world. The work of the church is not to instill the fear of what might happen to you after your death if you don't live the life of Love, the life of Jesus, Love's face, but only announcing the good news of what life is like in the present when you do.

This affirmation by the church of universal Love would help eliminate the danger of the sad and constant obsession with what will happen, what it will look like, when will it happen, and to whom it will happen. For many people it's a constant, paralyzing fear. Some church recruitment teams prey on this fear with questions like, "If you died tonight do you know where would will spend eternity?" or "Are you saved?," implying that God doesn't really Love us yet, and that maybe we haven't done something we're supposed to do to bring about our own trip safely to heaven after death, and if we don't do it God will "get" us. The assumption is that the goal of the Christian faith is not to Love your neighbor, but rather, to do whatever you have to do to get to heaven, as if it's not about your neighbor, it's about you. But universal Love for the other, beyond ourselves, is the whole point of the faith. (By the way, the correct answer to both questions above is "Yes!")

The proclamation of universal Love would help correct the impression held by many outside the Christian faith that church people are just looking out for themselves, and would do or say anything to escape death and hell or nothingness, to achieve a good end in heaven. In fact, we must admit that sometimes it's true. We must admit that even many Christians appear to want it so badly they would do anything to get it—join a church, memorize Bible verses by the score, even say they Love God, whatever the church wants them to say or do—anything to escape the death they fear and an uncertain eternity. But what we all need to hear, inside and outside the church, is that universal Love has already brought us home. It's already been decided and done. We are completely and fully Loved. All of us. No exclusions, anywhere, anyone.

Perfect Love leaves no one behind. It is not something to be possessed exclusively by anyone or any group. It is always proclaimed as universal, for all, and as such we are all one body in one whole global family, all of whom are children of God. If one person is in pain, we all are in pain; if one person hurts, we all hurt; if one person is hungry, we are all hungry. So it is with the Good News. If it is exclusionary, if just one person, or a few persons, or many persons are left out, it is *bad* news for the excluded, and because we are one body it is bad news for us all. For it would point to the failure of God's primary wish, Love's goal, that all people every-where would be brought back into the family of God's Love. The universality of salvation, the universality of the eternal life with God beyond this life, is Good News, because it is for all.

When children discover that they are unconditionally loved by their parents—not on the basis of how well they perform, not on the basis of what they believe, but just because they are their parents' own—then they thrive and grow and flower. *In the same way, as the church shows in its life and work that no one is excluded, that all people are God's people, God's children, that we are already fully totally Loved by God, a Loving Father, a Loving Mother, and that Love extends in all life and death and beyond, we are set free to grow and flower in our lives as well.* The fulfilled and joyful life in the present and in all life to come, is a gift from God, from Love itself, and yet it is so hard for us to stop trying to do something to get it, to deserve it. But it is not to be "gotten." It has always been there waiting to be discovered in the intentional living of the life of Jesus, the life of extending Love and care and kindness and justice and peace beyond ourselves wherever there is need.

This is what God wants for us, what Love demands, for us all: to turn away from constantly centering our lives on ourselves and our wants and needs; to be last in line, not first. In his letter to the Philippian church, Paul describes the Christian life by urging Christ's followers to think of others as *better* than themselves, and to "look not to your own interests, but to the interests of others."[22] In other versions, for example the RSV, translators decided on "look not *only* to your own interests, but *also* to the interests of others," a much softer version, and much easier to live with. But for Paul, "not looking to your own interests, but to the interests of others" is precisely the life to which he calls them in the very next sentence, when he urges them to "Let the same mind be in you that was in Christ Jesus," who was certainly not looking to his own interests *at all* as he approached the cross. He was looking *totally* and *only* to the interests of his followers. He gave his life

22. Philippians 2:1–11.

fully for others, nothing held back, and revealed the Love beyond which there is none greater. Those who are followers of Jesus, who are the face of God, the face of Love, are servants, not masters, not feeling they somehow need to work and strive for a successful and happy heavenly end for themselves. Servant living, trusting fully in patterns of kindness, compassion, justice, forgiveness, and sacrificial Love, throughout the human family and beyond, rather than living out a strategy to get to heaven, rises above all else, and enables us to live freely without any fearful future anticipation of an uncertain end. This is what God wants for all of us. This is how God created us to be.

But the question always comes up: What about Hitler? Is he going to be in heaven or is he already there? Or Kim Il Sung, or Osama Ben Laden, or Bernard Madoff, or the local public official who is taking kickbacks on contracts, or the lady down the street who poisons pets who come on her lawn, or the vindictive supervisor, or the local school crack salesman? How can we possibly say that these people, and so many others we can name, will be lifted up into the Loving, safe, eternal presence of God when the time arrives? How could God possibly Love these people that much? For that matter, how could God Love *me* that much? I mean, how can there be a precise breakpoint between God's embracing and rejecting without destroying Love's truth?

It isn't as if they and we appear before God, who then says, "It's all okay folks, I forgive you. You did bad, but let's just forget it." No, what is required is that we be changed, that we be repaired, recreated, made new to fit into God's new life of perfect Love.[23] This has been happening to us all our lives, in our encounters with the Holy, over and over, in moments large and small of Loving care and forgiveness and sacrifice and healing and justice finally established, as Love tries to gradually smooth away the rough edges of our lives in this world. We can't do it ourselves. It is God, it is Love, in the end, when all is done, who at last *finishes* the creation begun

23. See 1 Corinthians 15:51–57 for a first-century expression of this moment.

so long ago that dark night in the skies above Eden, a creation that even now continues to break into our lives when Love tears down a wall or recreates a life.

The leaves on the tree of life in the city of God that is to come are for the *healing* of the nations—all the nations, that is, everyone, to whom God sent Abraham.[24] This clearly means that people are going to need healing. People are not as they should be until they are made fit. God is at work in judgment, and this judgment means "making things right." That's what a judge does. A judgment sets things the way they are supposed to be, the right way, perhaps not perfect in human experience, but often the best a judge can do. The judgment of God, however, the presence of perfect Love, sets things fully right and perfect. In the life to come, in perfected Love, God's creative power brings about a healing, remaking us all, making us over (for we can't make ourselves over), making us right when we were wrong, making us acceptable when we were unacceptable, to the life of the Loving resurrection, ready for what we only caught a glimpse of in this life, a full, complete, and joyful life with God.

Without it, the Christian proclamation is bad news, as if a father or mother would say to a child, "I will love you deeply, I will give you good gifts, and I will care for you and comfort you in your time of trial, but only if you behave yourself and don't break any of the rules I set down for you, and say you're sorry for anything that goes wrong, and only if you tell me I am like God to you, and tell me how wonderful I am, and that you love me. But if you don't do those things, if you screw things up, if you hurt someone, or break something, or if you are ever less than Loving and caring and unselfish, then I will abandon you in a New York minute, and cause you to live in torture and pain for eternity."

Not a very healthy relationship for a parent and a child to have, nor is it a very happy relationship for God to have with us, God's own children. Rather, God says to all creation and every living being what parents say or need to say to their children: *"There is nothing you could ever do that would make me stop loving you. I*

24. Revelation 22:2b.

*may not always like what you do; I may even hate what you do. But
I will always Love you and embrace you as my own. I Love You. I
already Love You. I have always Loved you. I will always Love you."*

"Behold," says the Lord, "I make all things new."[25]

I've always thought Ben Franklin, in writing his epitaph, said it
very well:[26]

The body of

B. Franklin, Printer;

(Like the cover of an old book,

Its contents worn out

and stripped of its lettering and gilding)

Lies here, food for worms.

But the work shall not be lost:

For it will, (as he believed) appear once more,

In a new and more elegant edition,

Revised and corrected

By the Author.

This is what we pray for at Christmastime, when we sing the carol:[27]

Be near me Lord Jesus; I ask Thee to stay
Close by me forever, and love me, I pray.
Bless all the dear children in Thy tender care [that's all of us!]
And fit us for heaven, to live with Thee there.

For all of us on this green earth, and in the universe beyond, the
Love of God is too all-encompassing to end at death, or at any
religious or theological border, or at any other event in creation.
God's universal eternal Love should be a central affirmation of our
proclamation, for it is a joyful truth that we can be truly passionate
about! This gift of eternal life is what God freely gives to all of us. It
sets us free from the consuming attention to and fear of what will

25. Revelation 21:5.
26. Isaacson, *Franklin*, 470.
27. The Presbyterian Hymnal, 25.

ultimately happen to us in the end, so that we can faithfully live the life of Jesus here and now: the fulfilled life of sacrificial Love and servanthood, the best life there is, the life of true peace.

This is the Love that Will. Not. Let. Us. Go.

And, it sure will take a load off your mind!

10

A Kind of Finale

A clear and simple truth:
The Love that will not let us go

THE OTHER DAY, I went to the post office to pick up a package. As I was getting out of the car, I heard a voice weary and fragile call out, "Excuse me, could you help me get across the street to the bus stop? I'm not too steady on my feet." I turned to see a disheveled elderly woman over on the sidewalk in a worn cloth coat, carrying two paper shopping bags by their handles. But she wasn't calling to me. She was calling to a man who looked to be about seventeen, approaching her on a bicycle in the street. I thought at first he might be going by her, and I was about to offer help, when he stopped, put his bike down at the curb, and said to her, "*Of course* I'll help you."

In the days and weeks that now have followed this incident, I keep coming back to it, listening to it, reliving it, for it was important, and deserves attention. It is important because in that unselfish Loving act there on the sidewalk by the post office was a clear demonstration of the holy presence of Love, the voice of God who *is* Love itself, working itself out. It wasn't as dramatic as a soldier falling on a grenade to save his friends or a fireman running into a burning building to save a child. It didn't take long, and it will never be in the papers or the nightly newscast or on CNN online. But it is one of the multitude of events just like it, all around us every day, that have the power to touch our hearts and point to what is really important in human life. It is repeated literally everywhere. It was one of God's countless gifts of Love to the woman, to the man, to me, to others who heard it, and now to you. I have no idea whether or not the young man or the elderly woman ascribed to any church or theology or religious system. In my mind, and I expect in theirs, it didn't even come up. Love superseded all that. Love had its own voice. Love came first.

This book has been about the Christian faith in its simplest form, and perhaps a somewhat different way to talk about it. It is a Christian proclamation that I believe is uncomplicated, makes sense, touches and excites the heart, and inspires the mind (rather than occasionally doing battle with it).

The central truth of Christianity is the recognition that God is Love. They are the same, and when we experience Love we experience God. The Christian life is simply the celebration, living, and giving away countless gifts of Love, the holy Love that is all around us and works in and through us. It is not a destructive, selfish, mean-spirited, controlling love, but a Love that grasps your heart and often takes your breath away; a Love that defines life's purpose, and enlightens our daily journey. It is a Love shared and given away; it is the Love of the servant.

We see it happening on sidewalks next to post offices, in hospitals, in offices, at construction sites, on farms, in living rooms, in bedrooms, in restaurants, in schools, in jails, in neighborhoods, wherever there is human community. We experience it, we lose it, we want it, we remember it, we yearn for it, we mess it up, we twist it for our own purposes. Some of us can't remember ever knowing it, and some of us even despise it. But in its presence, or at those times it seems absent, for good or ill, right or wrong, Love is the most vital determining element in every life.

Christians affirm that God is the origin and the creator of Love, as well as its presence, and many people are drawn to God by seeing and experiencing Love or the lack of it or the confusion about it in their lives. Others read and listen to the stories about Love and grace that fill the Bible, and as the Spirit (God's breath) reaches out to them through those pages, as they link it up to the Love they have already discovered or yearn for in their own lives. Some get sidetracked by trying to find out whatever they can *about* God—whether God really exists, takes up space, has weight and mass, that sort of thing. Some spend a lot of time trying to figure out how to control Love, or to be God in their own lives and set their own destinies, or to figure out how all those miracles in the Bible really happened, and how they can get to heaven when they die.

But when the Spirit touches you, when Love breathes on and in you, when you come to *know* God by knowing Love, rather than just attempting to know *about* God, *about* Love, those issues are no longer important, and often disappear entirely. When you find yourself overwhelmed by Love, what you are really overwhelmed by is God. *It's very simple: God is Love; Love is God.*

God is always there for you, just as God was there for the woman outside the post office. Let me rephrase that sentence: *Love* is always there for you, just as *Love* was there for the woman outside the post office. Moments and events like these drive us together with others who have experienced this breathtaking Love, and to a new vision of the church, where unconditional, universal, sacrificial, forgiving Love is nurtured and celebrated as the very presence of God, and the central point of its life and proclamation.

If you consider yourself non-religious or "unaffiliated" (and have read this far!), then you should know that if you have ever been overwhelmed by Love in any of its forms, then you are already one of us. Christianity's bottom line is not about whether you believe that something is true *about* God or Jesus or the Spirit, or what doctrines are right or wrong, or whether you will go to heaven when you die. Scores of Christians believe differently on these subjects, and although it would be nice if we were all of one mind about all that, well, that hasn't happened yet. It would also be nice if everyone who was a church member or affiliated with religion in some form never did anything wrong or anything they were or should be ashamed of, or never made a bad decision, or never hurt each other, but, well, that hasn't happened yet either. We are wounded and our eyes are indeed clouded in many ways.

The Christian faith is about discovering, beyond our human weaknesses and failings, the Love that God wants for us anyway. Go back now to chapter 4 and reread those accounts of Love happening—the elderly couple, the two deacons, the mother and her daughter, and the others—and then look back and recall your own stories. Think back, remember them, and watch for new ones happening right now. They're all around you. They are the voice of God.

Machiavelli said that it is better to be feared than to be Loved, but he was wrong. Love may not always lead to power as the world defines it, but perfect Love is God's answer to fear and does truly cast it out. God spoke this Love in Jesus, the human face of God, the human face of Love. In his life, death, and resurrection, Love explodes into our lives, awakening us to a compelling, breathtaking joy that has always been there pounding on our hearts' doors since the beginning. It is this transforming Love that we receive and give away that enables us to walk through the dark valleys of hurt and pain and evil. It is a Love—because it is God—that does not end, ever, and in this Love, death shall be no more. This great Love—because it is God—is for *all* of us, freely given, without exception, without exclusion, for all time and beyond.

If you really want to get your life together, don't be overcome trying to figure out complex "churchy" theological language (at least at first). *Being Christian is not what you think, it's what you do.* Theological ideas and categories may help you as time goes by, and the Christian story certainly will, but these things aren't primary. Instead become engaged in some form of Love, especially sacrificial Love, a Love in which you have to give something up. This means lives of falling on grenades, running into burning buildings, helping people across the street, working for the establishment of homes for children living on the streets around the world, feeding the hungry, being with the lonely, healing the sick, building hospitals and clinics where there is need but no money, visiting people in nursing homes who have no family, taking a walk with a grieving friend, and all the rest. All this is what Christians mean when they say "Follow Jesus" or "Love Jesus." This is where you will discover what you're looking for.

You know what you are to do and be; you know already. It's written on your heart. God has already put it there. You discover it and recognize it in the life and face of Jesus where Love is uncovered and made visible for you. You find it in overwhelming moments of Love and kindness and giving yourself to the needs of another. It is a revelation, an uncovering for you, as you are awakened to the presence of Love itself, and Love's countless gifts. Love has always been there, and when you catch sight of it, and feel it, then you are set free from less significant concerns so you can begin to live that way. Listen for it. It's not all that complicated. It's very simple. It's right there, right in front of you. And it makes perfect sense.

The uncomplicated, unvarnished truth of the Christian faith, Christianity in its simplest form, is living, celebrating, and extending Love through all creation—Love that is persistent, unceasing, unconditional, undeserved, uninterrupted, eternal, universal, forgiving, healing, and sacrificial. Love runs through all life and experience like an overflowing nourishing river from God's own garden. Many hide from it in shallows and eddies, but once it sweeps you away—and it will—your life will never be the same. Like a Loving father, like a Loving mother, this is what God wants for all people, "all the dear children," all of us.

This is the Love that will never let us go.

Bibliography

Bowie, Beverley. "Memorandum on Mortality." In *Know All Men by These Presents*, by Beverley Bowie, 19–21. New York: Bookman Associates, 1958.

Forbis, Wesley, editor. *The Baptist Hymnal.* Nashville: Convention Press, 1991.

Grenz, Stanley J., and Roger E. Olson. *Who Needs Theology?: An Invitation to the Study of God.* Downers Grove, IL: InterVarsity, 1996.

Isaacson, Walter. *Benjamin Franklin: An American Life.* New York: Simon & Schuster, 2003.

Meacham, Jon. *Thomas Jefferson: The Art of Power.* New York: Random House, 2012.

North American Lutheran Church. "Confession of Faith." Online: http://thenalc.org/confession-of-faith/.

Pew Forum on Religion & Public Life. "Faith in Flux: Changes in Religious Affiliation in the U.S." April 2009. Washington, DC: Pew Research Center, 2009. Online: http://www.pewforum.org/files/2009/04/fullreport.pdf.

———. "'Nones' on the Rise: One-in-Five Adults Have No Religious Affiliation." October 9, 2012. Washington, DC: Pew Research Center, 2012. Online: http://www.pewforum.org/files/2012/10/NonesOnTheRise-full.pdf.

———. "U.S. Religious Landscape Survey: Religious Affiliation: Diverse and Dynamic." February 2008. Washington, DC: Pew Research Center, 2008. Online: http://www.pewforum.org/files/2013/05/report-religious-landscape-study-full.pdf.

———. "U.S. Religious Landscape Survey: Religious Beliefs and Practices: Diverse and Politically Relevant." June 2008. Washington, DC: Pew Research Center, 2008. Online: http://www.pewforum.org/files/2008/06/report2-religious-landscape-study-full.pdf.

Presbyterian Church (U.S.A.). *Book of Confessions.* Louisville, KY: Office of the General Assembly of the Presbyterian Church (U.S.A.), 2012.

———. *The Presbyterian Hymnal.* Richmond, VA: John Knox, 1990.

Smith, H. Shelton, et. al, *American Christianity, Volume II,* New York, Charles
   Scribner's Sons, 1963.
United Methodist Church. *The Book of Discipline of the United Methodist
   Church.* Nashville, TN: United Methodist Publishing House, 2012.